T0084157

GRAPHIC BIOGRAPHIES

William Penn

FOUNDER of PENNSYLVANIA

by Ryan Jacobson
illustrated by Tim Stiles

Consultant:
Dr. Craig Horle
co-editor of *The Papers of William Penn*
Temple University
Philadelphia

Capstone
press
Mankato, Minnesota

Graphic Library is published by Capstone Press,
1710 Roe Crest Drive, North Mankato, Minnesota 56003.
www.capstonepub.com

Library of Congress Cataloging-in-Publication Data
Jacobson, Ryan.
William Penn: Founder of Pennsylvania/ by Ryan Jacobson; illustrated by Tim Stiles.
p. cm.—(Graphic library. Graphic biographies)
Summary: "In graphic novel format, tells the story of Quaker leader William Penn, founder of the Pennsylvania Colony, whose ideas about government influenced the U.S. Constitution"—Provided by publisher.
Includes bibliographical references and index.
ISBN-13: 978-0-7368-6501-2 (hardcover)
ISBN-10: 0-7368-6501-2 (hardcover)
ISBN-13: 978-0-7368-9665-8 (softcover pbk.)
ISBN-10: 0-7368-9665-1 (softcover pbk.)
1. Penn, William, 1644–1718—Juvenile literature 2. Pioneers—Pennsylvania—Biography—Juvenile literature. 3. Quakers—Pennsylvania—Biography—Juvenile literature. 4. Pennsylvania—History—Colonial period, ca. 1600–1775—Juvenile literature. I. Stiles, Tim (Timothy) II. Title. III. Series.
F152.2.J33 2007
974.8'02092—dc22 2006006401

Designers
Jason Knudson and Thomas Emery

Colorist
Benjamin Hunzeker

Editor
Christine Peterson

Printed in the United States 5973

Table of Contents

Chapter 1
Becoming a Quaker

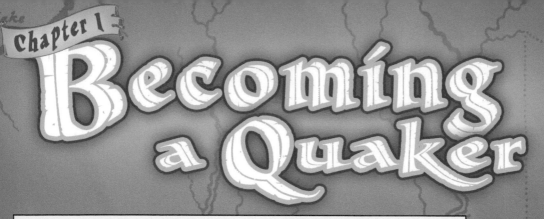

In 1656, 12-year-old William Penn lived with his family in Ireland. He was a religious boy who spent hours every day reading the Bible.

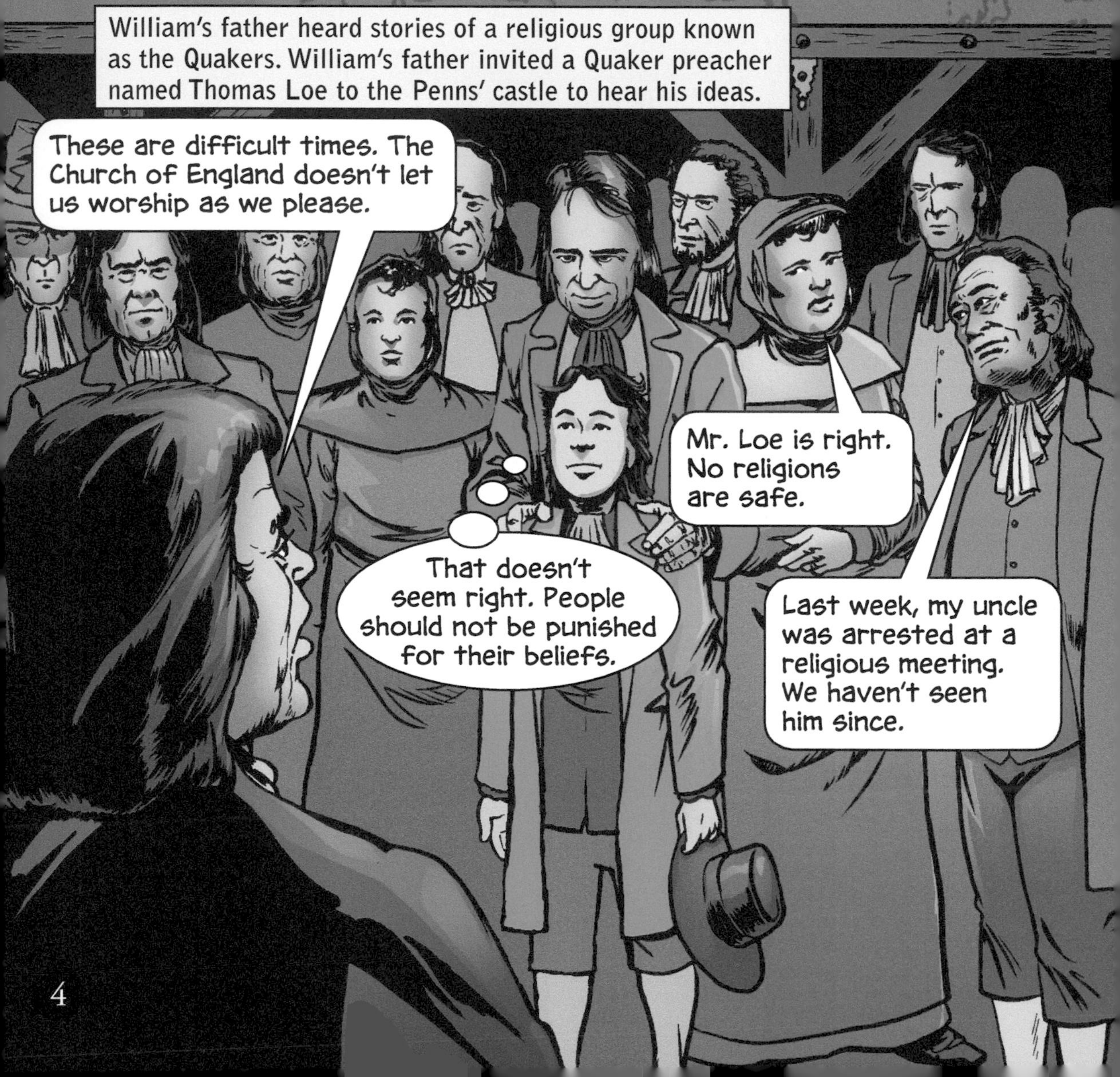
William's father heard stories of a religious group known as the Quakers. William's father invited a Quaker preacher named Thomas Loe to the Penns' castle to hear his ideas.
These are difficult times. The Church of England doesn't let us worship as we please.
Mr. Loe is right. No religions are safe.
That doesn't seem right. People should not be punished for their beliefs.
Last week, my uncle was arrested at a religious meeting. We haven't seen him since.

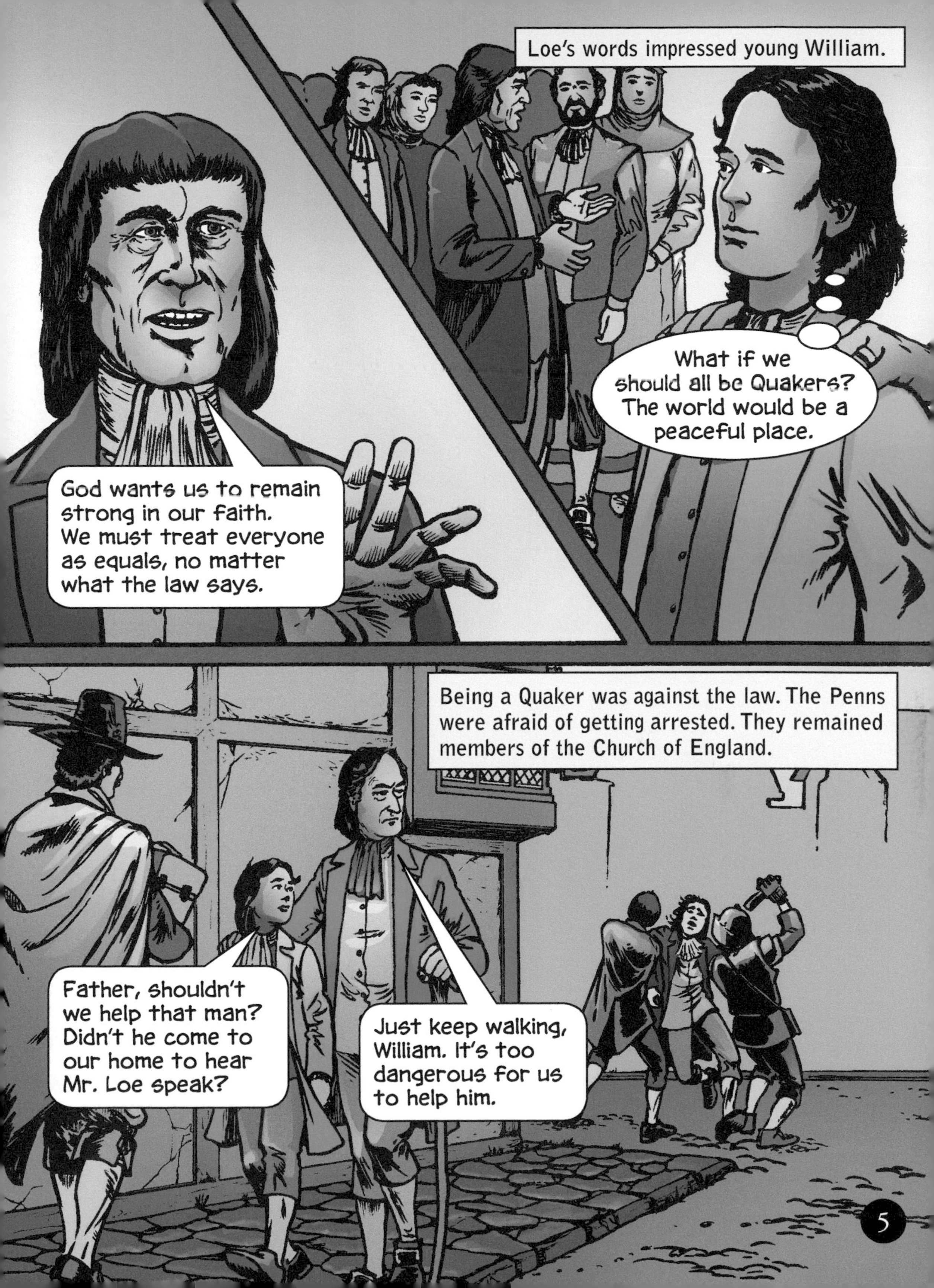
Loe's words impressed young William.
God wants us to remain strong in our faith. We must treat everyone as equals, no matter what the law says.
What if we should all be Quakers? The world would be a peaceful place.
Being a Quaker was against the law. The Penns were afraid of getting arrested. They remained members of the Church of England.
Father, shouldn't we help that man? Didn't he come to our home to hear Mr. Loe speak?
Just keep walking, William. It's too dangerous for us to help him.

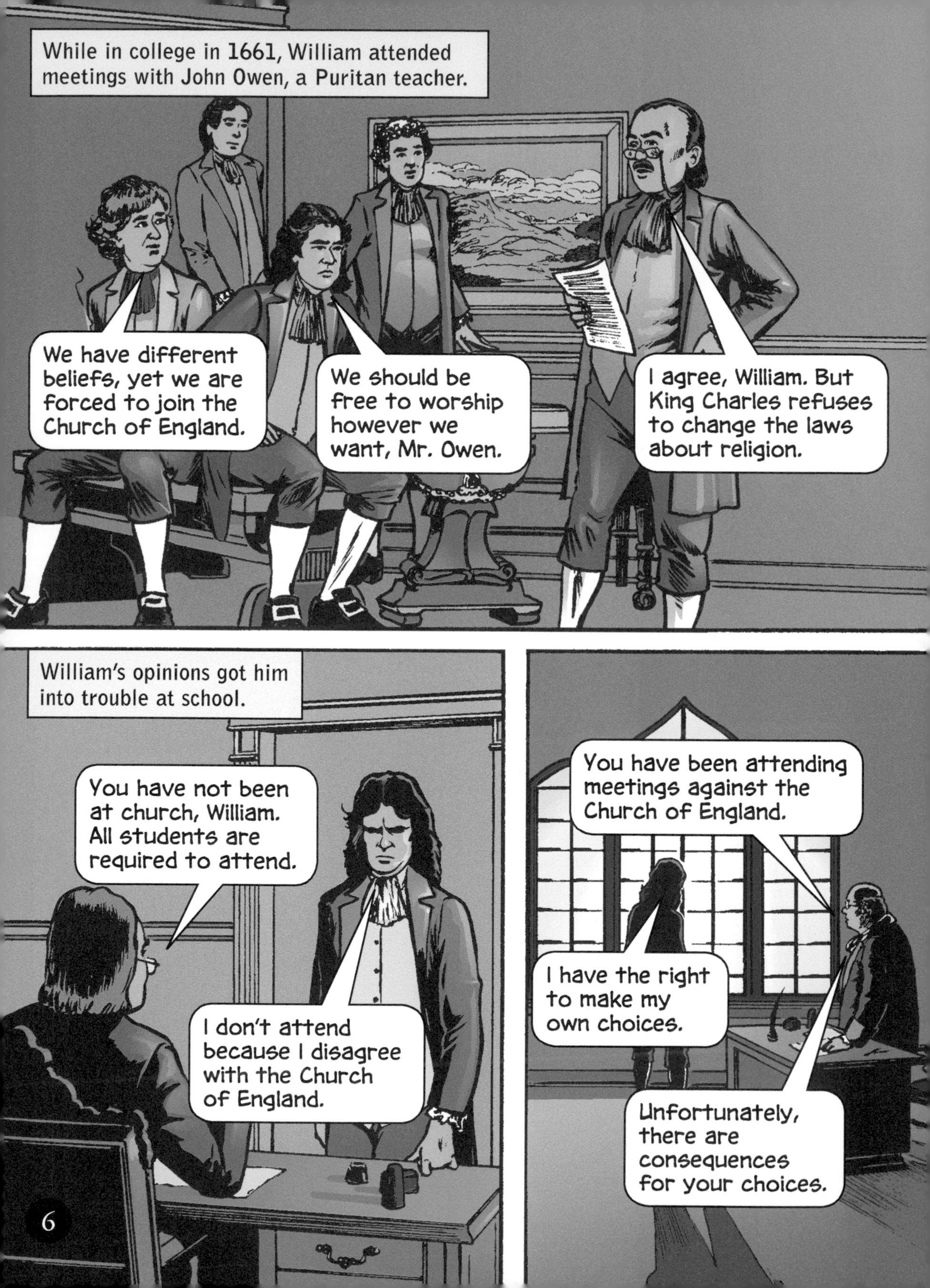
While in college in 1661, William attended meetings with John Owen, a Puritan teacher.
We have different beliefs, yet we are forced to join the Church of England.
We should be free to worship however we want, Mr. Owen.
I agree, William. But King Charles refuses to change the laws about religion.
William's opinions got him into trouble at school.
You have not been at church, William. All students are required to attend.
I don't attend because I disagree with the Church of England.
You have been attending meetings against the Church of England.
I have the right to make my own choices.
Unfortunately, there are consequences for your choices.

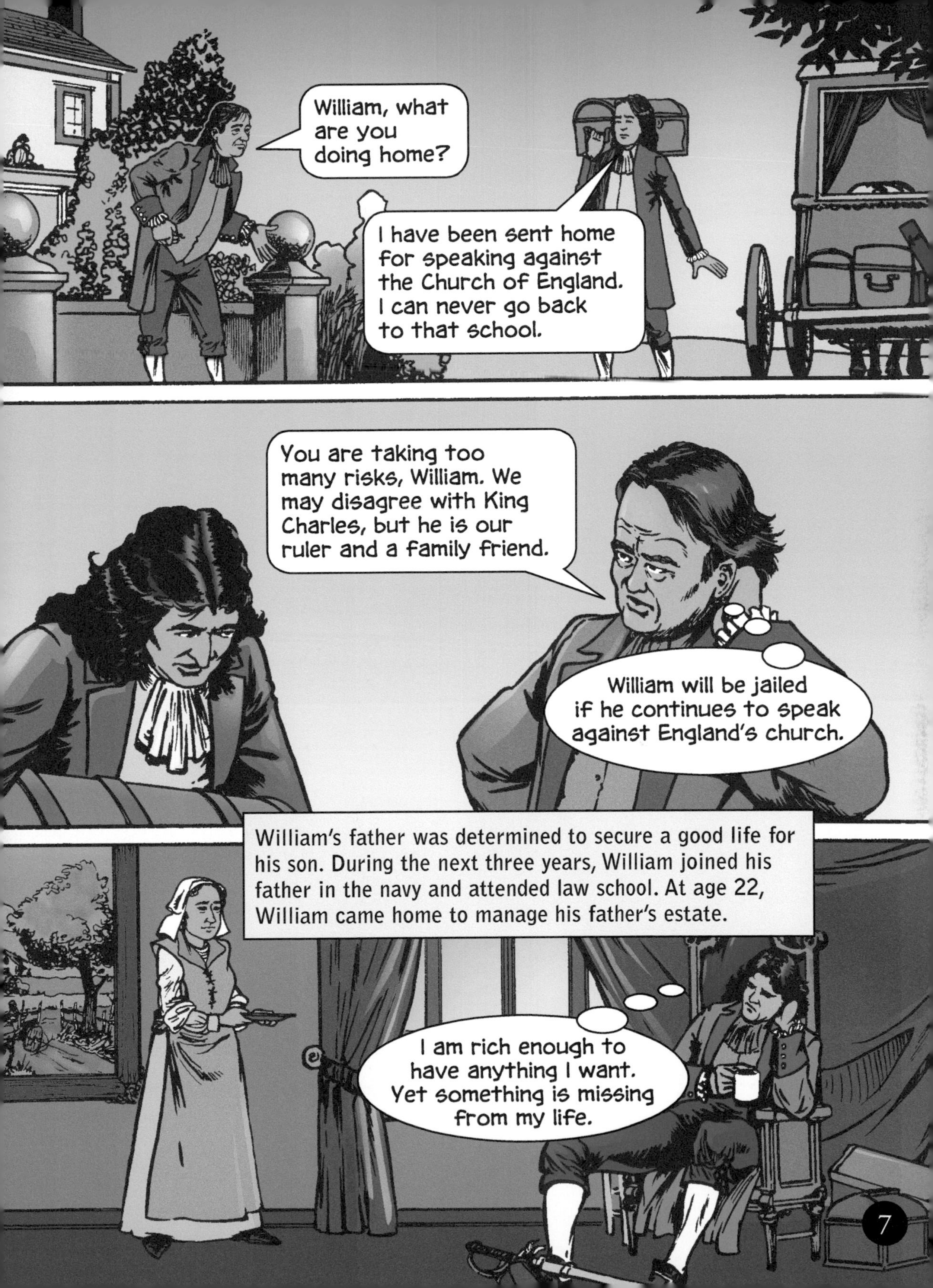
William, what are you doing home?
I have been sent home for speaking against the Church of England. I can never go back to that school.
You are taking too many risks, William. We may disagree with King Charles, but he is our ruler and a family friend.
William will be jailed if he continues to speak against England's church.
William's father was determined to secure a good life for his son. During the next three years, William joined his father in the navy and attended law school. At age 22, William came home to manage his father's estate.
I am rich enough to have anything I want. Yet something is missing from my life.

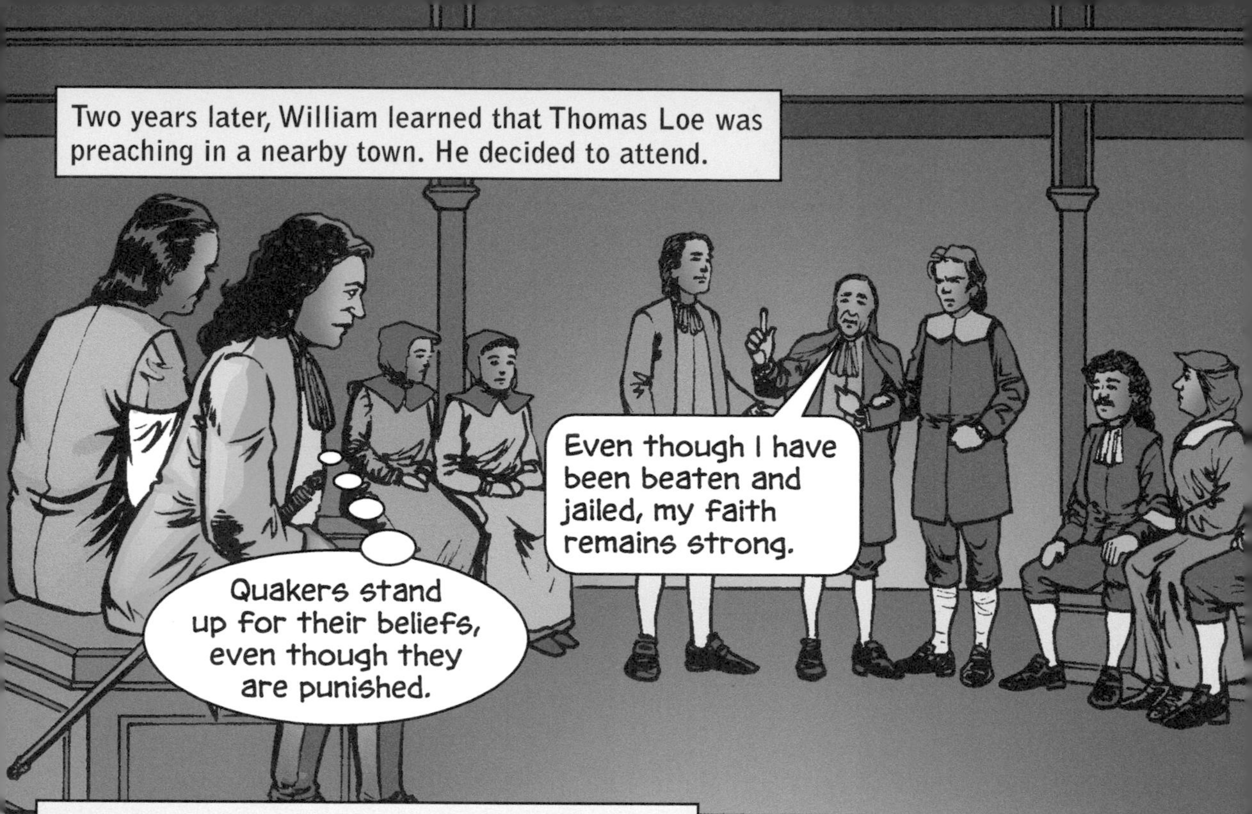
Two years later, William learned that Thomas Loe was preaching in a nearby town. He decided to attend.
Even though I have been beaten and jailed, my faith remains strong.
Quakers stand up for their beliefs, even though they are punished.

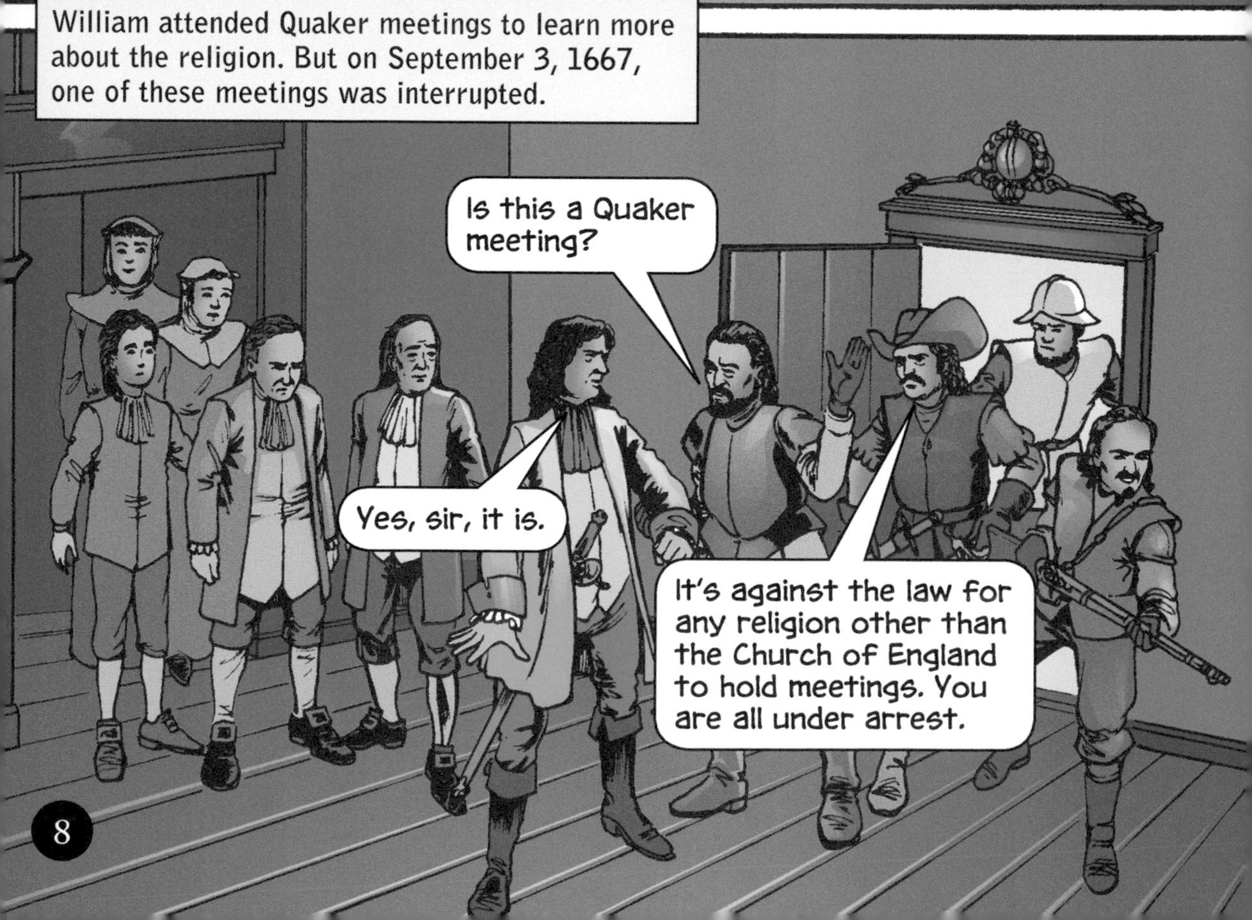
William attended Quaker meetings to learn more about the religion. But on September 3, 1667, one of these meetings was interrupted.
Is this a Quaker meeting?
Yes, sir, it is.
It's against the law for any religion other than the Church of England to hold meetings. You are all under arrest.

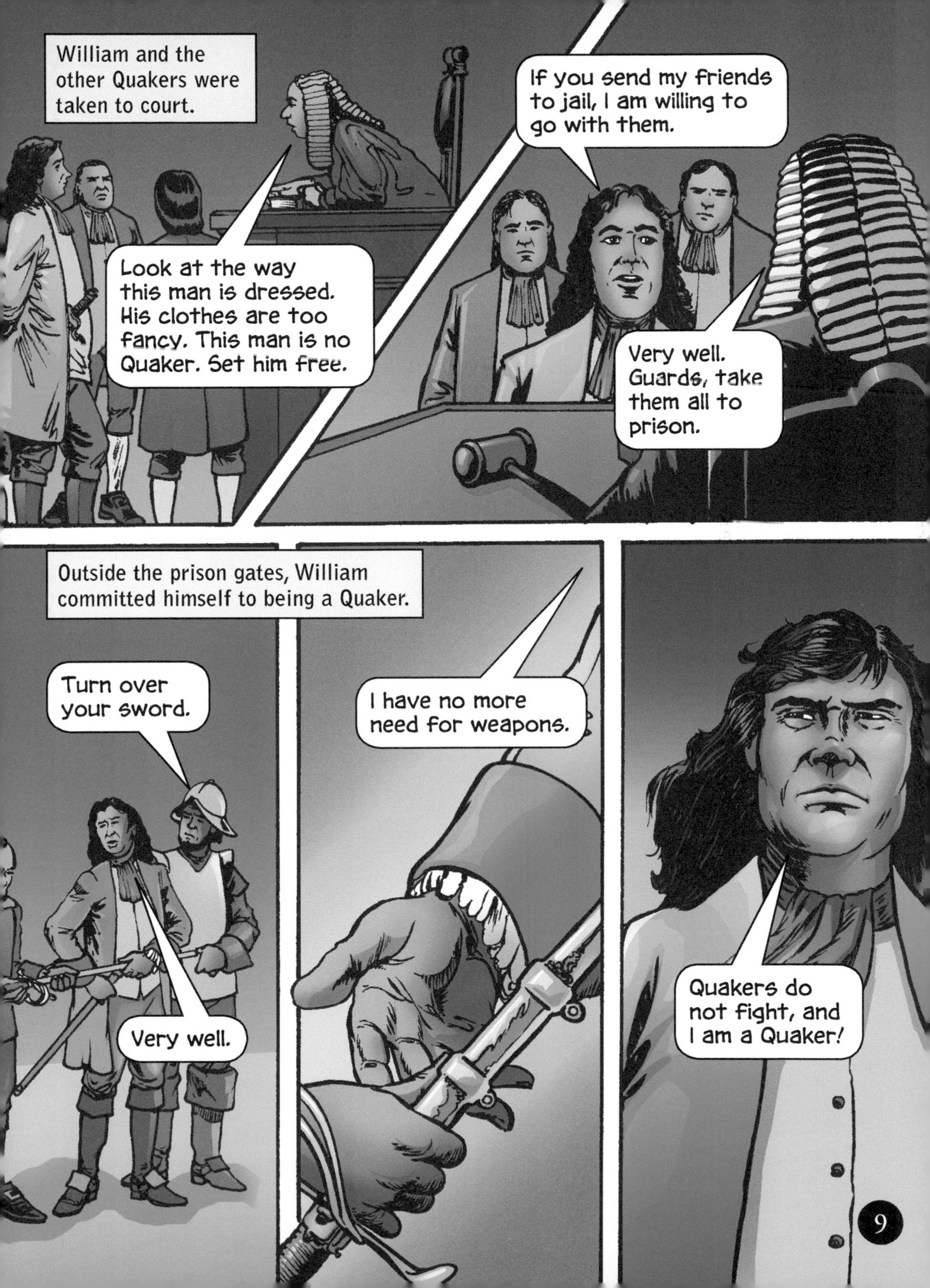
William and the other Quakers were taken to court.
Look at the way this man is dressed. His clothes are too fancy. This man is no Quaker. Set him free.
If you send my friends to jail, I am willing to go with them.
Very well. Guards, take them all to prison.
Outside the prison gates, William committed himself to being a Quaker.
Turn over your sword.
Very well.
I have no more need for weapons.
Quakers do not fight, and I am a Quaker!

Chapter 2
Land of the Free

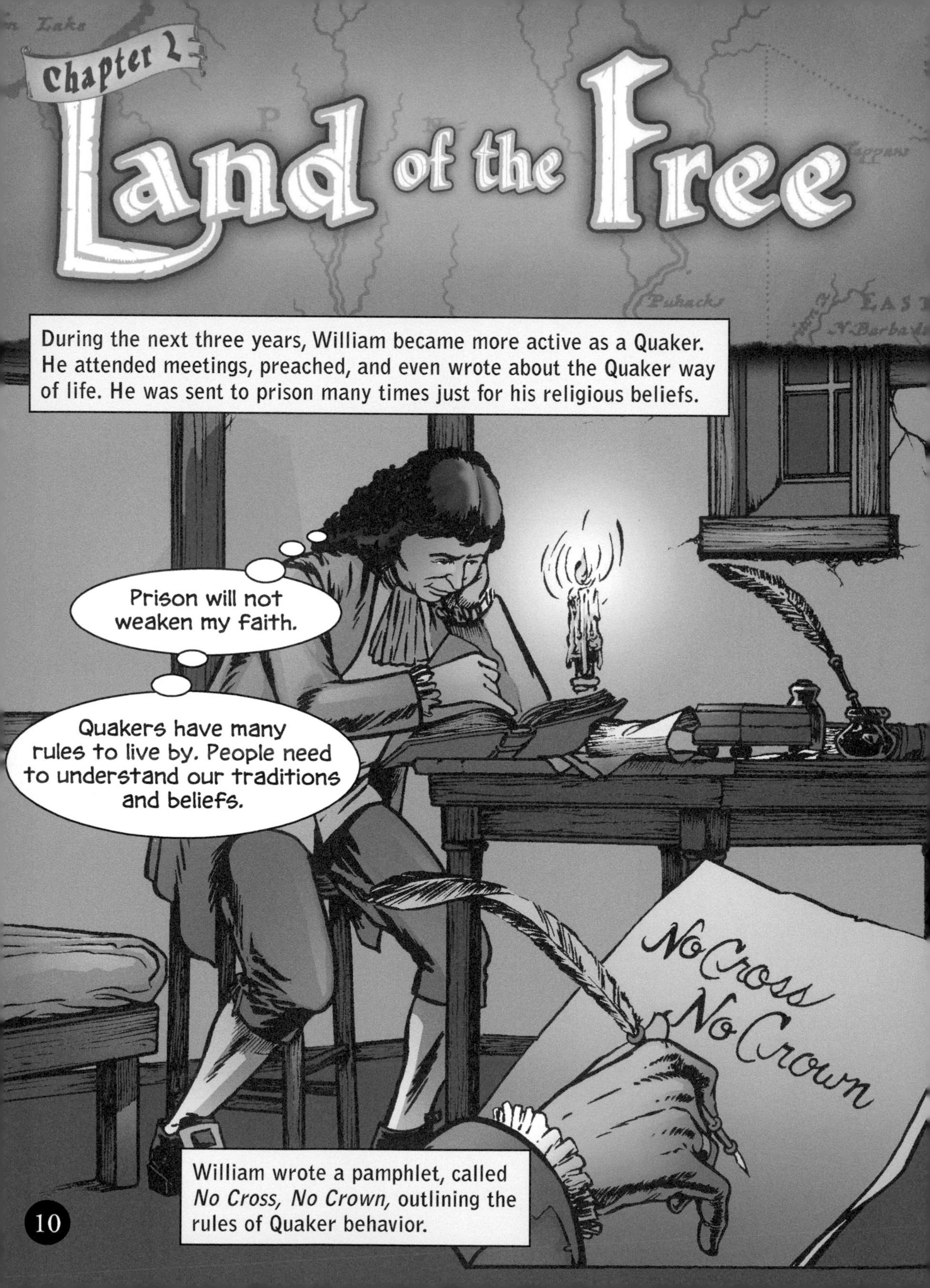

During the next three years, William became more active as a Quaker. He attended meetings, preached, and even wrote about the Quaker way of life. He was sent to prison many times just for his religious beliefs.
Prison will not weaken my faith.
Quakers have many rules to live by. People need to understand our traditions and beliefs.
No Cross No Crown
William wrote a pamphlet, called *No Cross, No Crown,* outlining the rules of Quaker behavior.

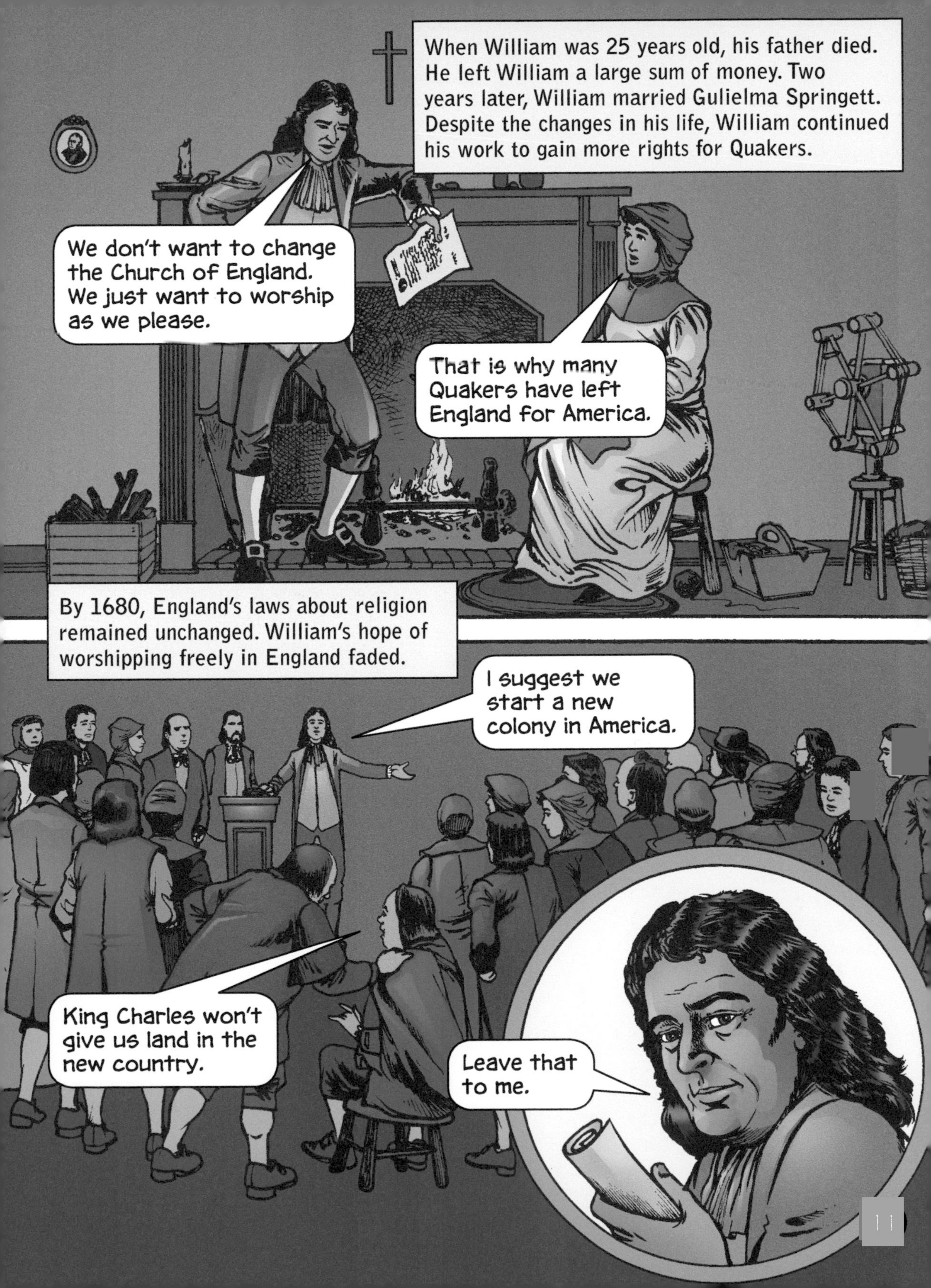
When William was 25 years old, his father died. He left William a large sum of money. Two years later, William married Gulielma Springett. Despite the changes in his life, William continued his work to gain more rights for Quakers.
We don't want to change the Church of England. We just want to worship as we please.
That is why many Quakers have left England for America.
By 1680, England's laws about religion remained unchanged. William's hope of worshipping freely in England faded.
I suggest we start a new colony in America.
King Charles won't give us land in the new country.
Leave that to me.

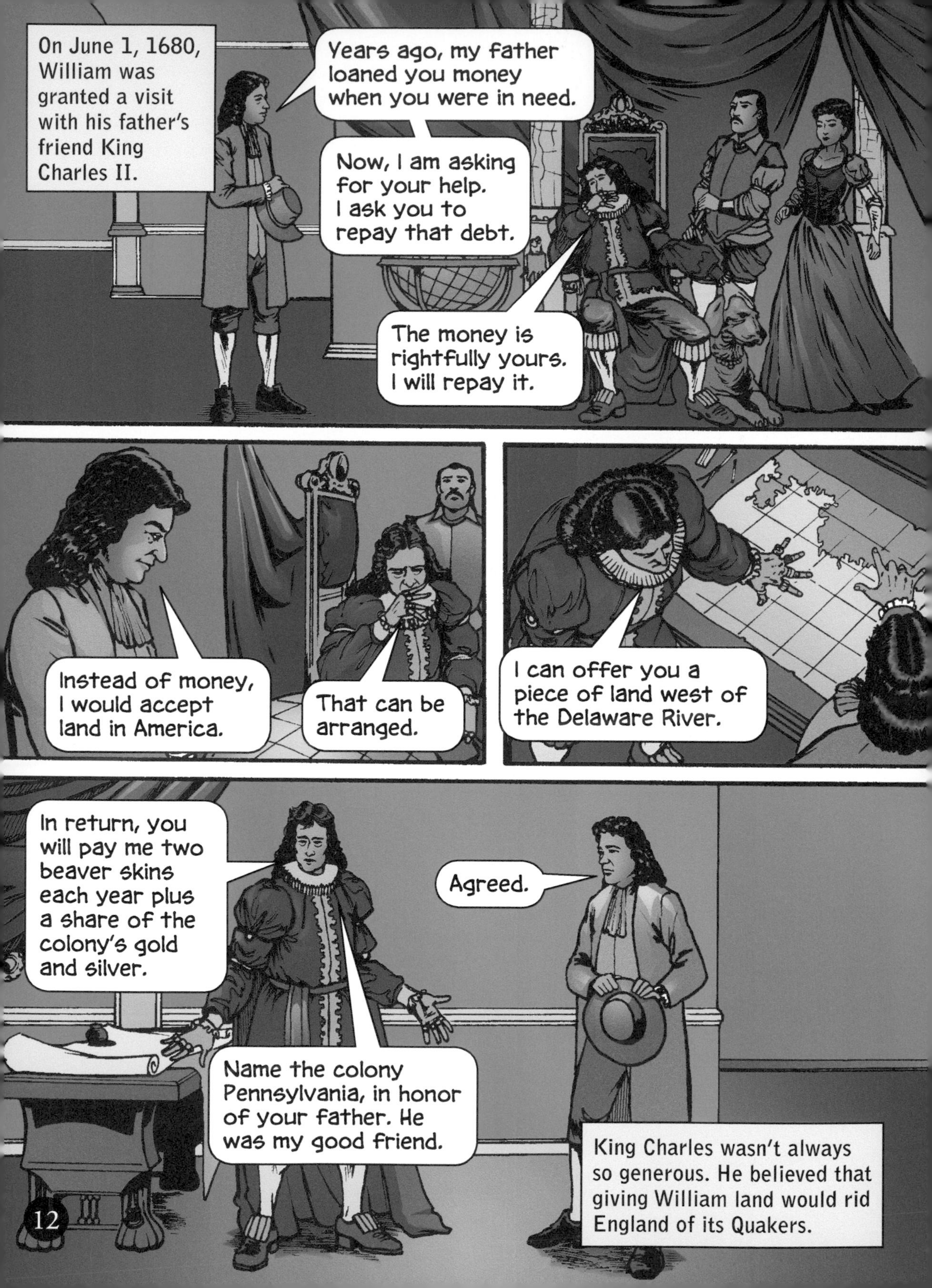
On June 1, 1680, William was granted a visit with his father's friend King Charles II.
Years ago, my father loaned you money when you were in need.
Now, I am asking for your help. I ask you to repay that debt.
The money is rightfully yours. I will repay it.
Instead of money, I would accept land in America.
That can be arranged.
I can offer you a piece of land west of the Delaware River.
In return, you will pay me two beaver skins each year plus a share of the colony's gold and silver.
Agreed.
Name the colony Pennsylvania, in honor of your father. He was my good friend.
King Charles wasn't always so generous. He believed that giving William land would rid England of its Quakers.

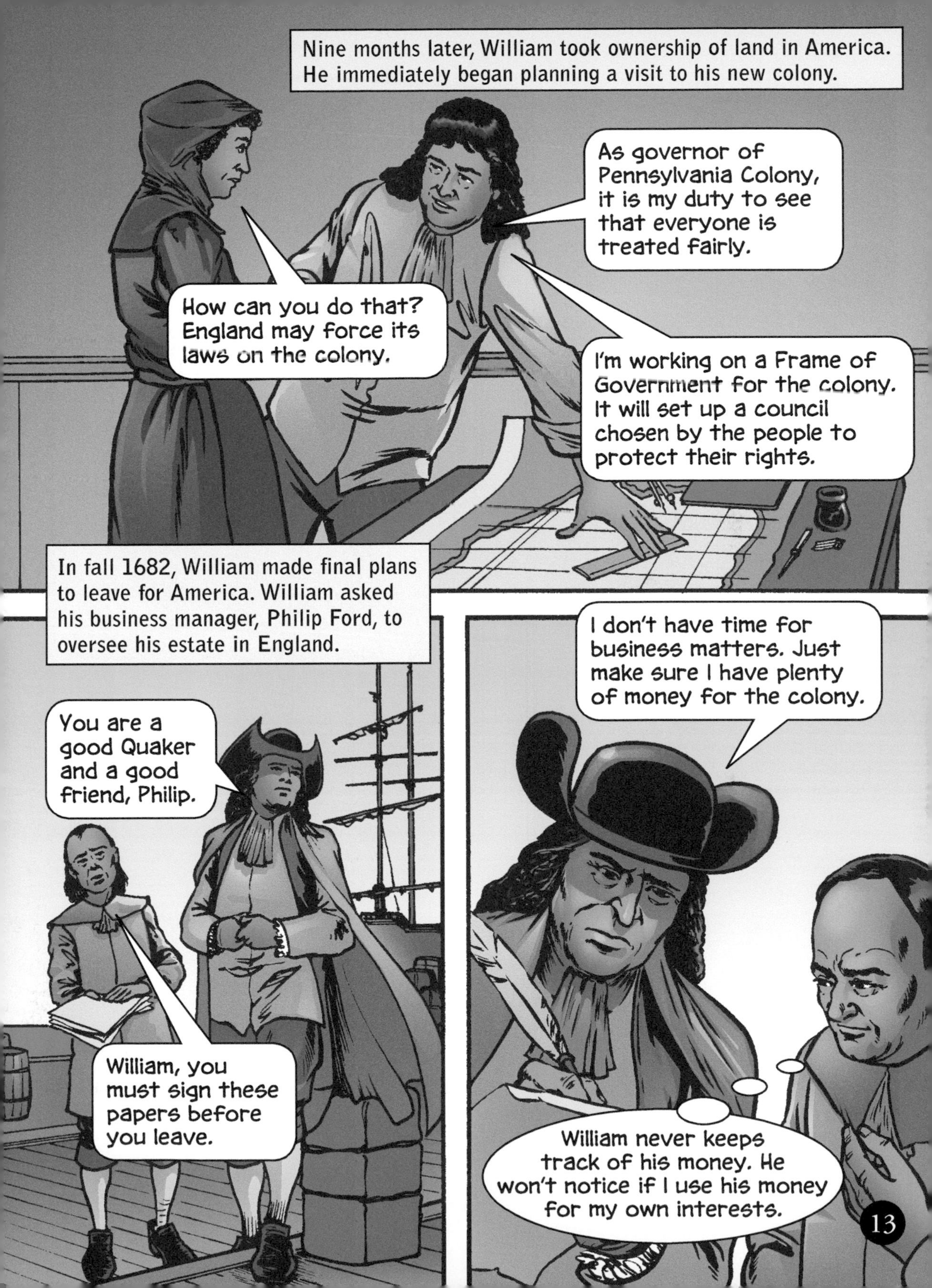
Nine months later, William took ownership of land in America. He immediately began planning a visit to his new colony.
As governor of Pennsylvania Colony, it is my duty to see that everyone is treated fairly.
How can you do that? England may force its laws on the colony.
I'm working on a Frame of Government for the colony. It will set up a council chosen by the people to protect their rights.
In fall 1682, William made final plans to leave for America. William asked his business manager, Philip Ford, to oversee his estate in England.
You are a good Quaker and a good friend, Philip.
William, you must sign these papers before you leave.
I don't have time for business matters. Just make sure I have plenty of money for the colony.
William never keeps track of his money. He won't notice if I use his money for my own interests.

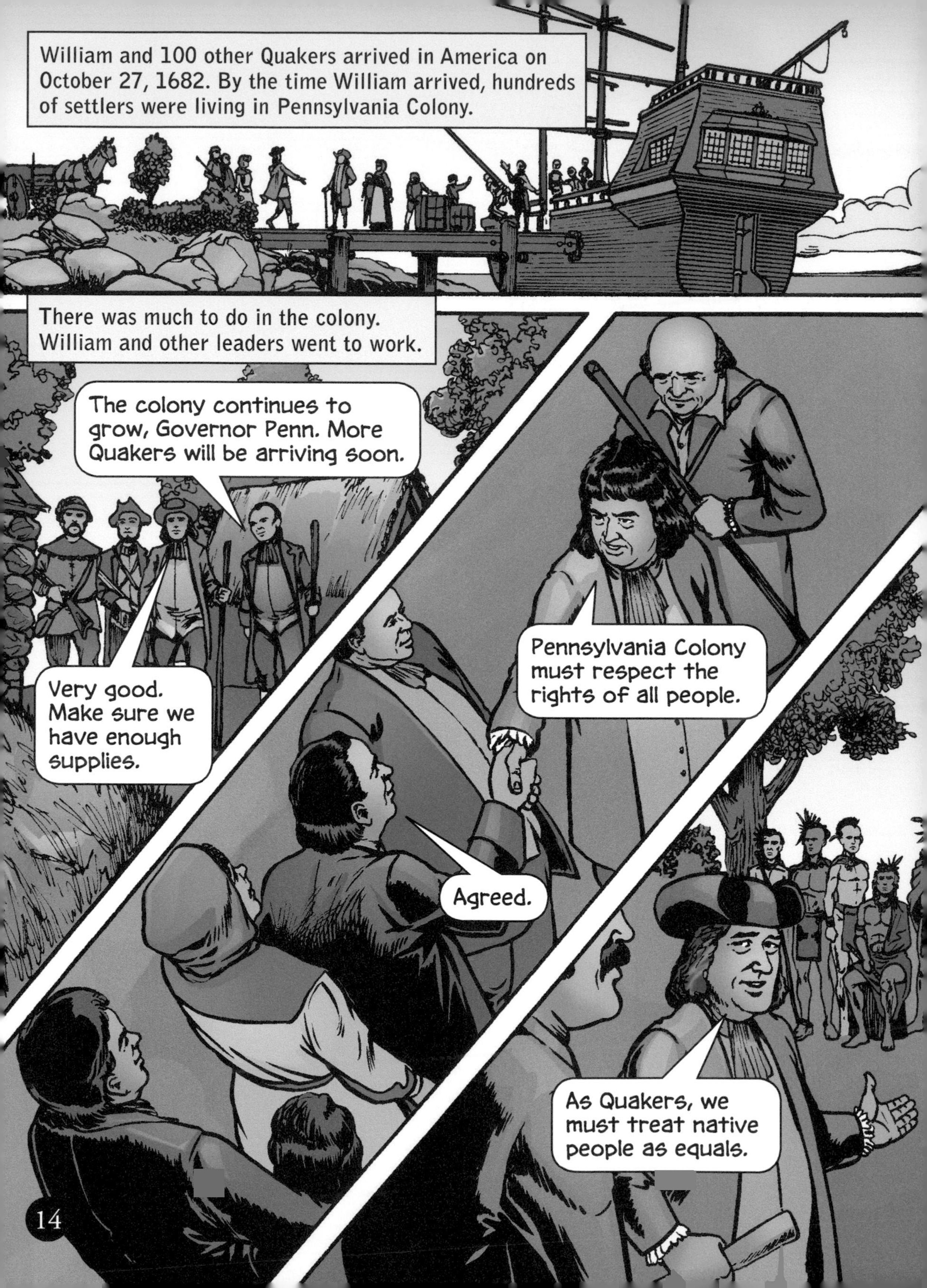
William and 100 other Quakers arrived in America on October 27, 1682. By the time William arrived, hundreds of settlers were living in Pennsylvania Colony.
There was much to do in the colony. William and other leaders went to work.
The colony continues to grow, Governor Penn. More Quakers will be arriving soon.
Very good. Make sure we have enough supplies.
Pennsylvania Colony must respect the rights of all people.
Agreed.
As Quakers, we must treat native people as equals.

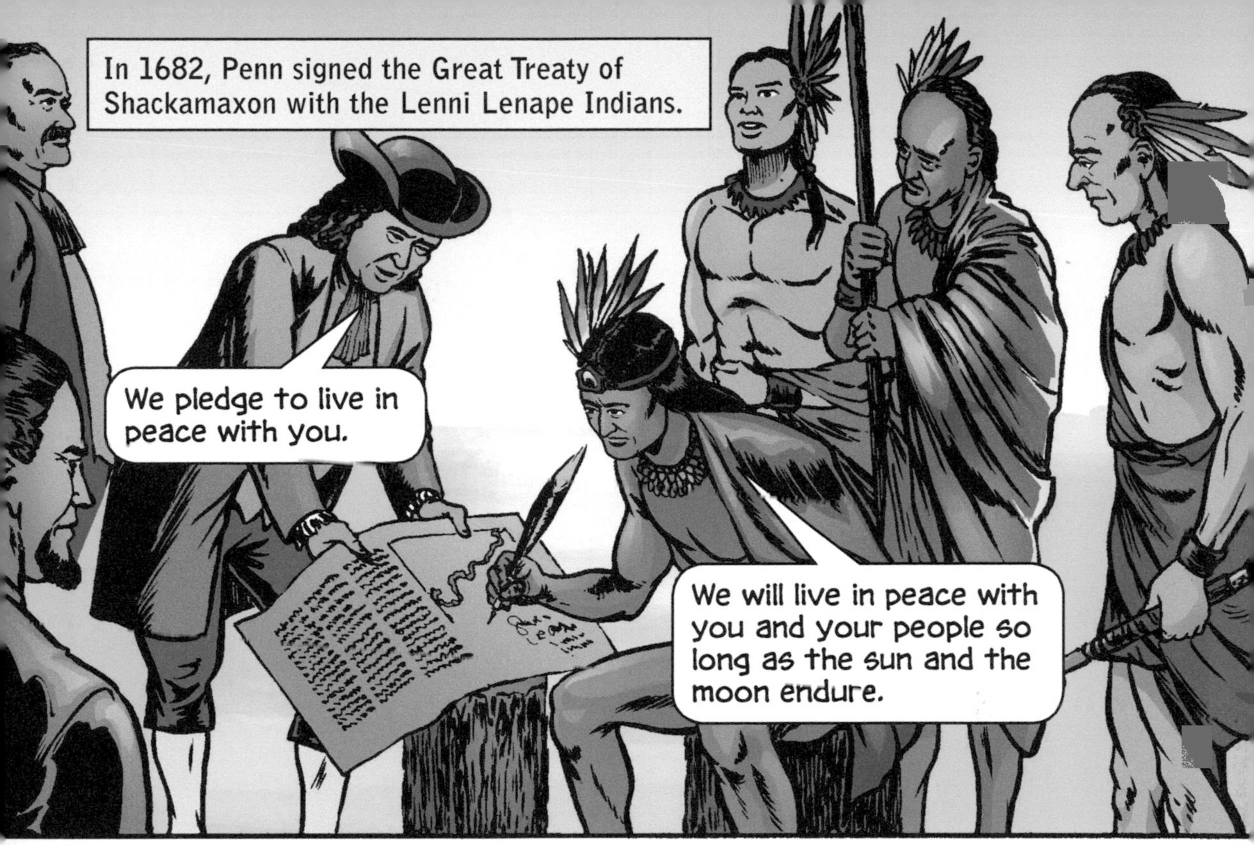
In 1682, Penn signed the Great Treaty of Shackamaxon with the Lenni Lenape Indians.
We pledge to live in peace with you.
We will live in peace with you and your people so long as the sun and the moon endure.

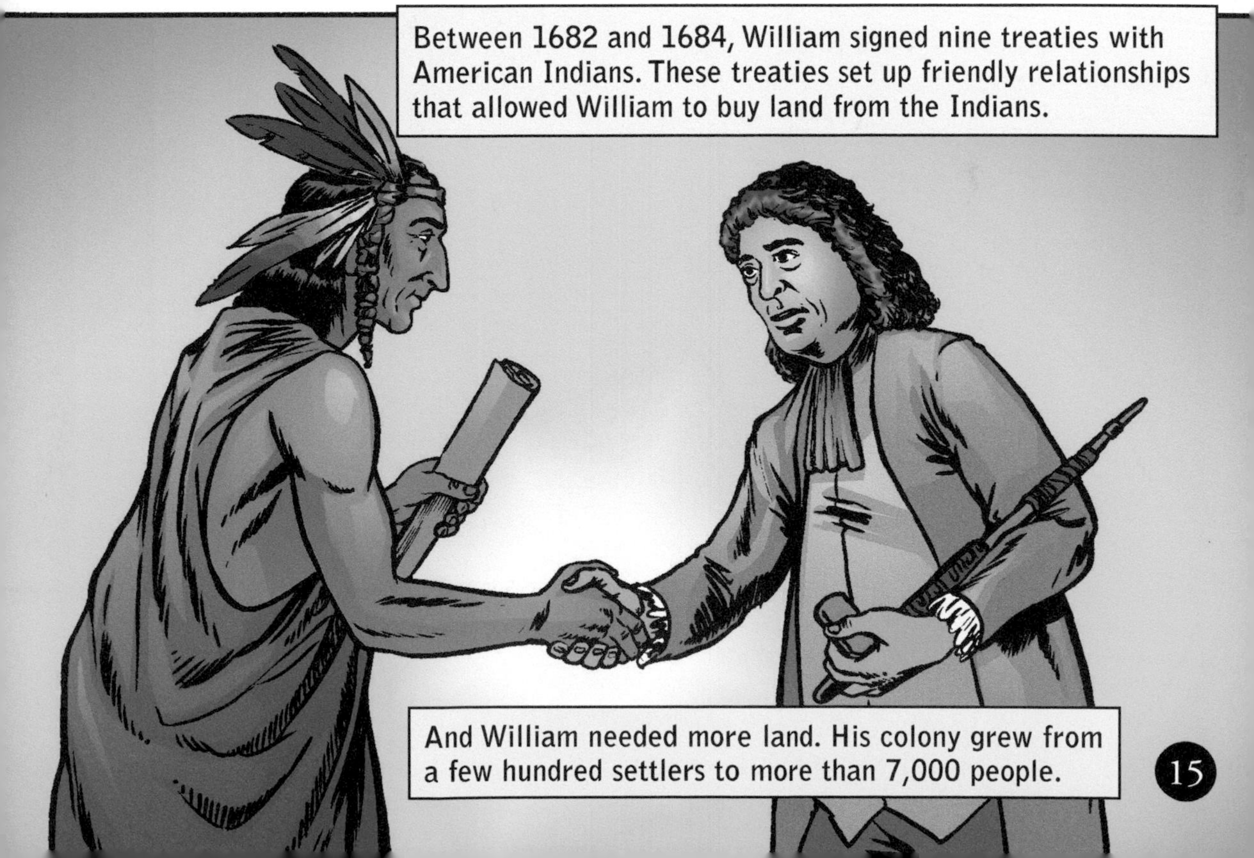
Between 1682 and 1684, William signed nine treaties with American Indians. These treaties set up friendly relationships that allowed William to buy land from the Indians.
And William needed more land. His colony grew from a few hundred settlers to more than 7,000 people.

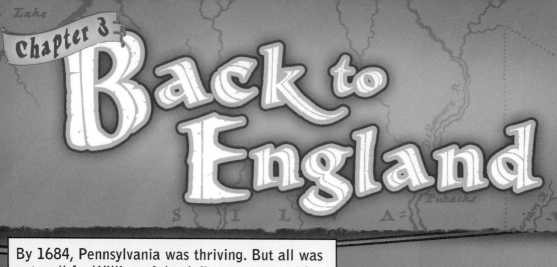

Chapter 3 Back to England

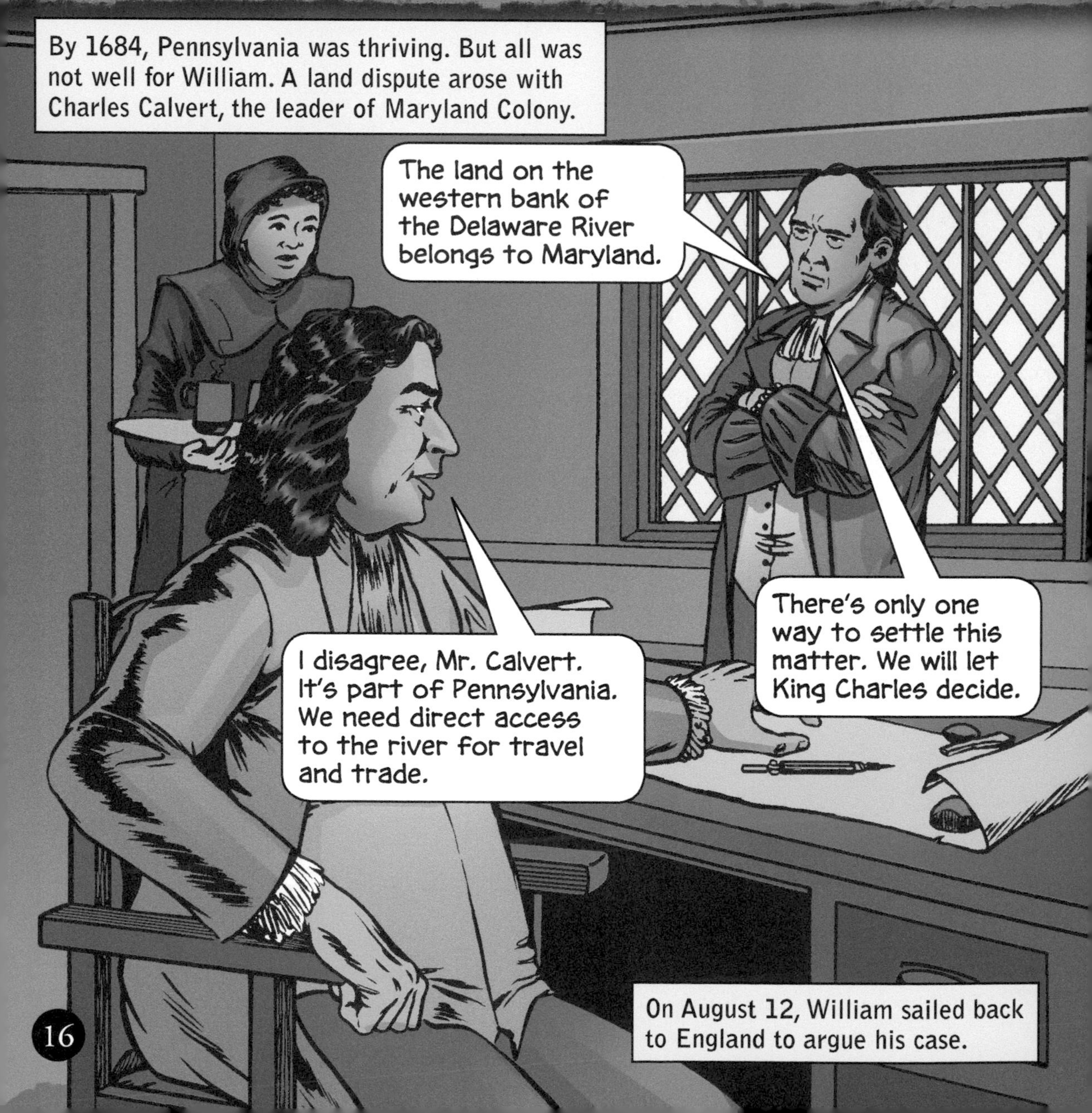
By 1684, Pennsylvania was thriving. But all was not well for William. A land dispute arose with Charles Calvert, the leader of Maryland Colony.
The land on the western bank of the Delaware River belongs to Maryland.
I disagree, Mr. Calvert. It's part of Pennsylvania. We need direct access to the river for travel and trade.
There's only one way to settle this matter. We will let King Charles decide.
On August 12, William sailed back to England to argue his case.

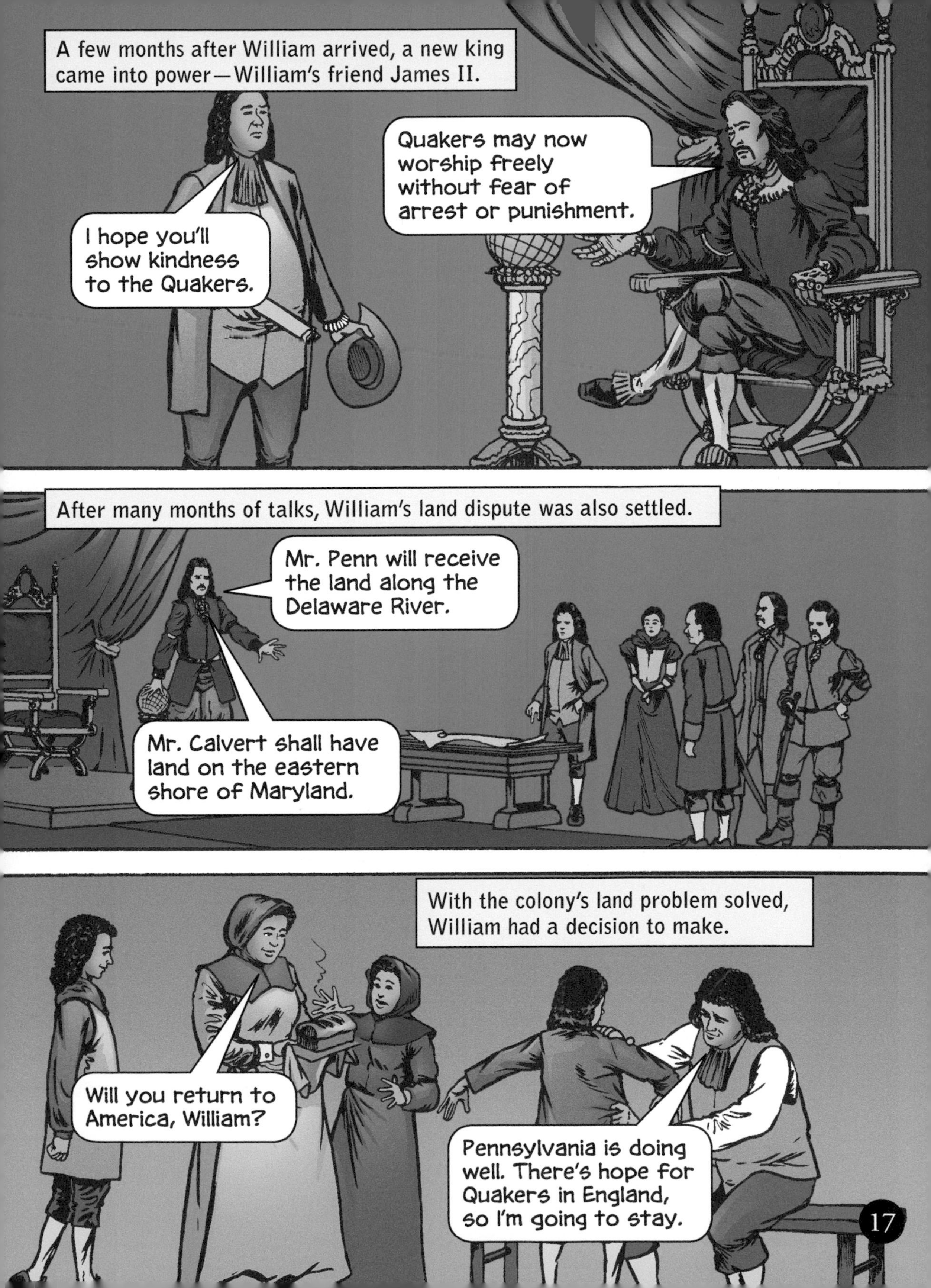
A few months after William arrived, a new king came into power—William's friend James II.
I hope you'll show kindness to the Quakers.
Quakers may now worship freely without fear of arrest or punishment.
After many months of talks, William's land dispute was also settled.
Mr. Penn will receive the land along the Delaware River.
Mr. Calvert shall have land on the eastern shore of Maryland.
With the colony's land problem solved, William had a decision to make.
Will you return to America, William?
Pennsylvania is doing well. There's hope for Quakers in England, so I'm going to stay.

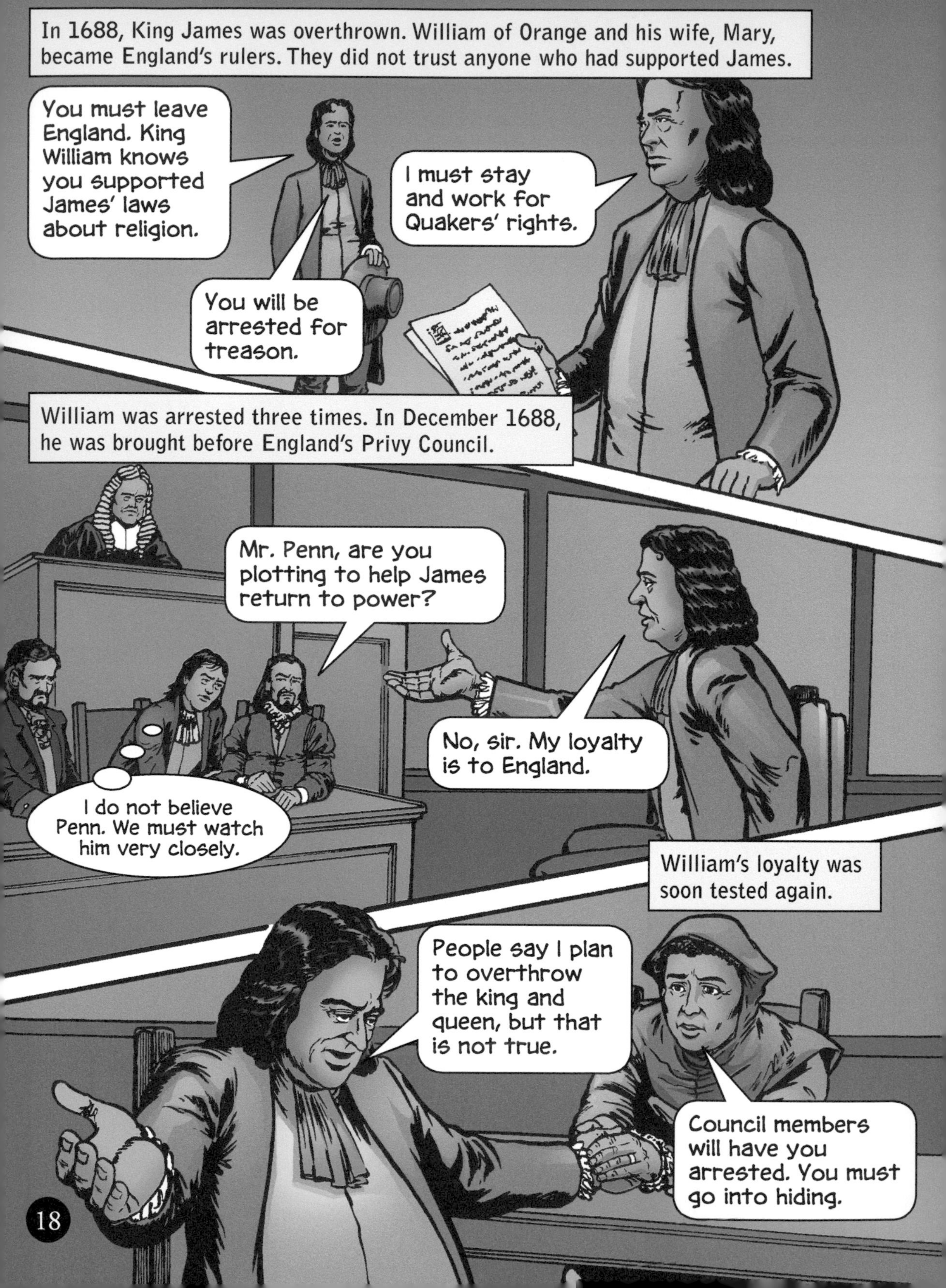
In 1688, King James was overthrown. William of Orange and his wife, Mary, became England's rulers. They did not trust anyone who had supported James.
You must leave England. King William knows you supported James' laws about religion.
I must stay and work for Quakers' rights.
You will be arrested for treason.
William was arrested three times. In December 1688, he was brought before England's Privy Council.
Mr. Penn, are you plotting to help James return to power?
No, sir. My loyalty is to England.
I do not believe Penn. We must watch him very closely.
William's loyalty was soon tested again.
People say I plan to overthrow the king and queen, but that is not true.
Council members will have you arrested. You must go into hiding.

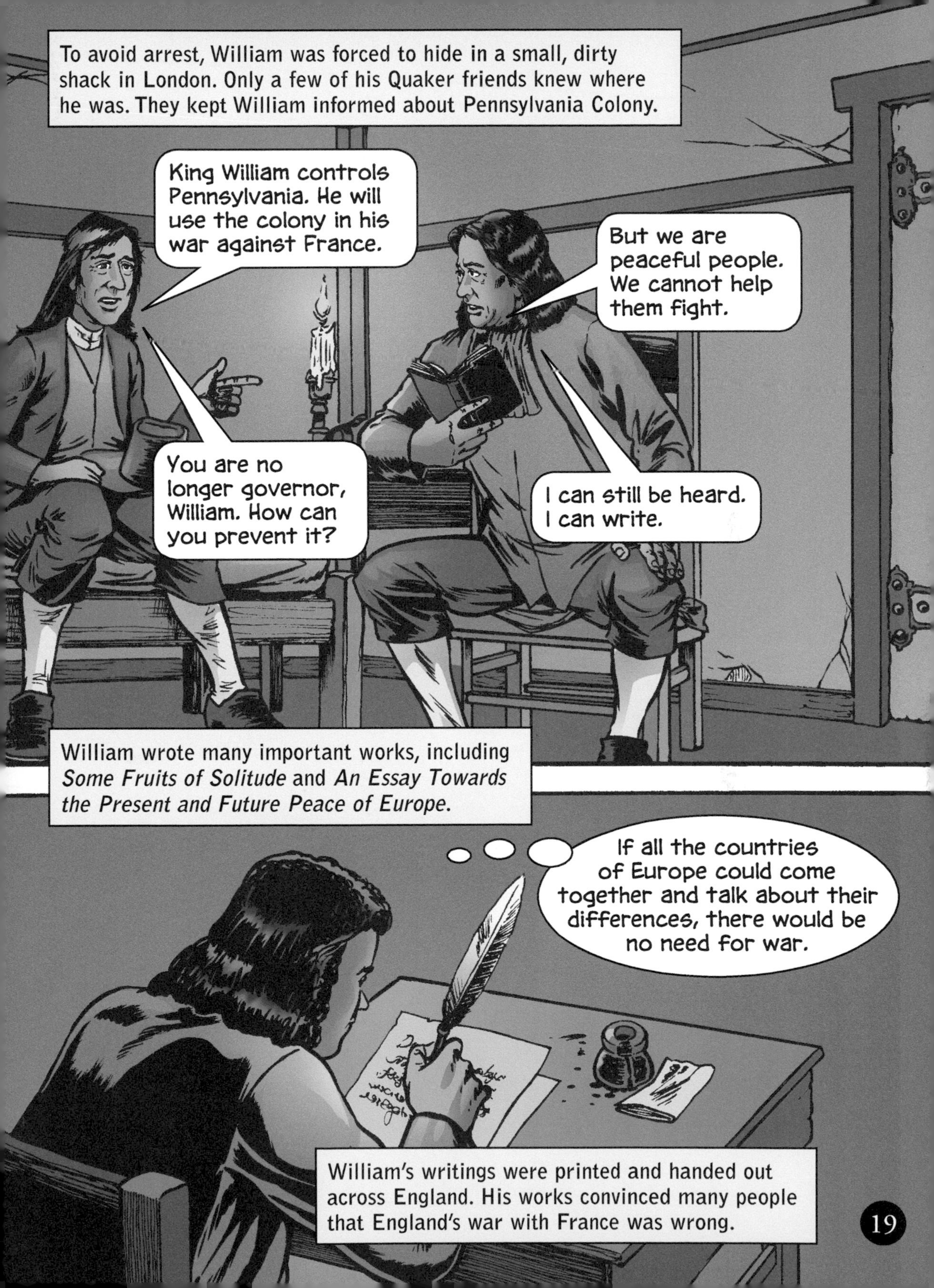
To avoid arrest, William was forced to hide in a small, dirty shack in London. Only a few of his Quaker friends knew where he was. They kept William informed about Pennsylvania Colony.
King William controls Pennsylvania. He will use the colony in his war against France.
But we are peaceful people. We cannot help them fight.
You are no longer governor, William. How can you prevent it?
I can still be heard. I can write.
William wrote many important works, including Some Fruits of Solitude and An Essay Towards the Present and Future Peace of Europe.
If all the countries of Europe could come together and talk about their differences, there would be no need for war.
William's writings were printed and handed out across England. His works convinced many people that England's war with France was wrong.

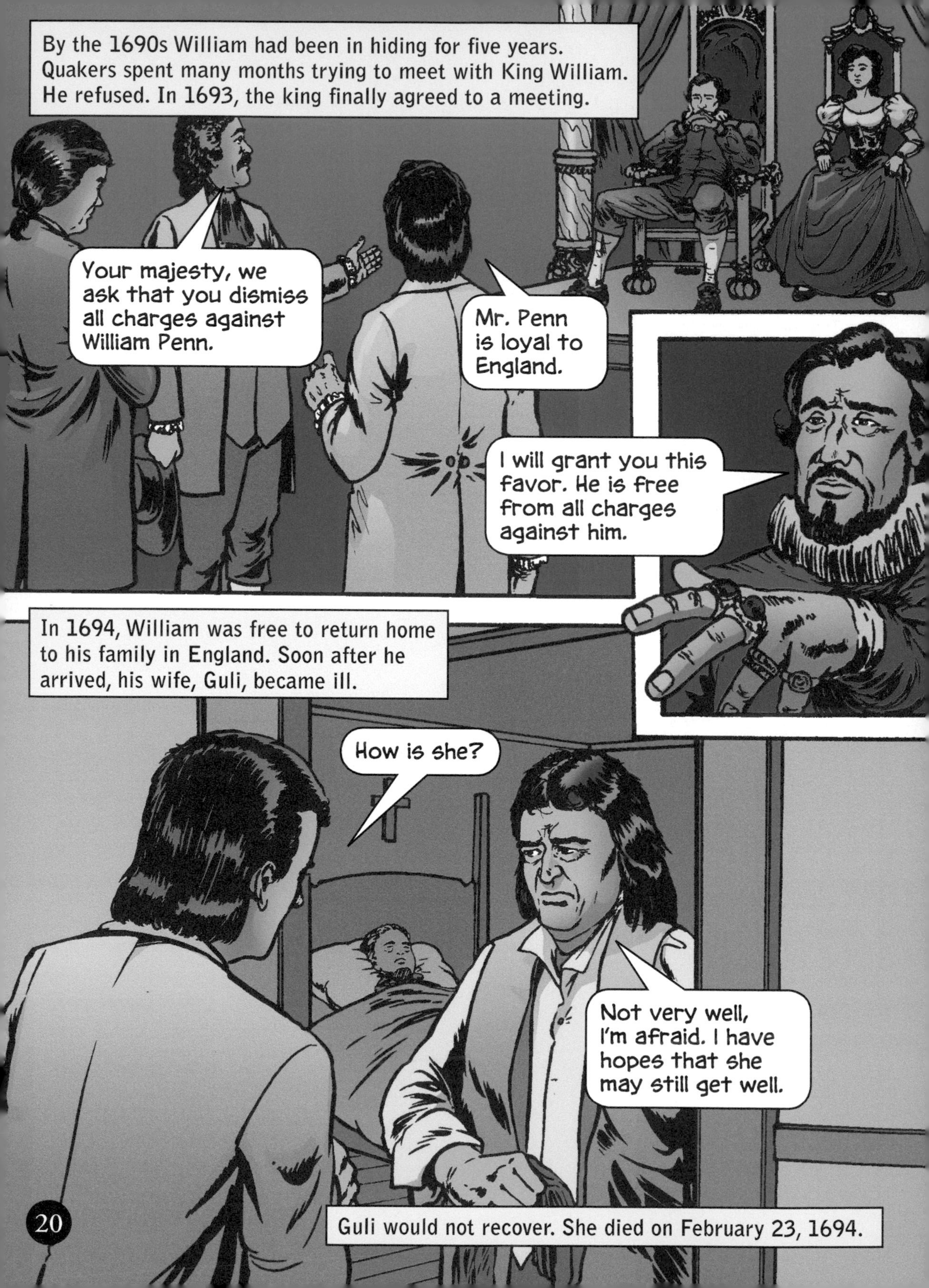
By the 1690s William had been in hiding for five years. Quakers spent many months trying to meet with King William. He refused. In 1693, the king finally agreed to a meeting.
Your majesty, we ask that you dismiss all charges against William Penn.
Mr. Penn is loyal to England.
I will grant you this favor. He is free from all charges against him.
In 1694, William was free to return home to his family in England. Soon after he arrived, his wife, Guli, became ill.
How is she?
Not very well, I'm afraid. I have hopes that she may still get well.
Guli would not recover. She died on February 23, 1694.

Despite his sadness, William worked to get his colony back from English control.

Pennsylvania has not helped England in its war against France. I ask that you return the colony's ownership to me.

It shall be done only if you return there and serve as governor.

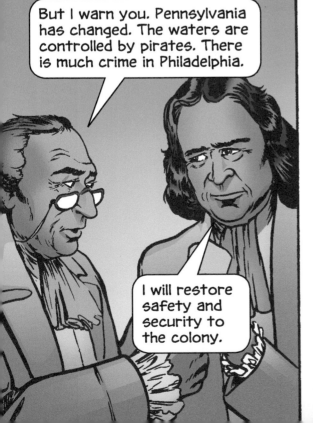

But I warn you. Pennsylvania has changed. The waters are controlled by pirates. There is much crime in Philadelphia.

I will restore safety and security to the colony.

Before he left England, William married Hannah Callowhill. On September 3, 1699, William and his family set sail for America.

21

Chapter 4
The Last Trip Home

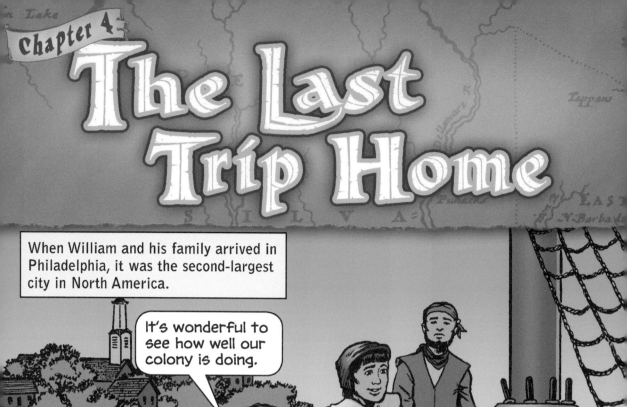

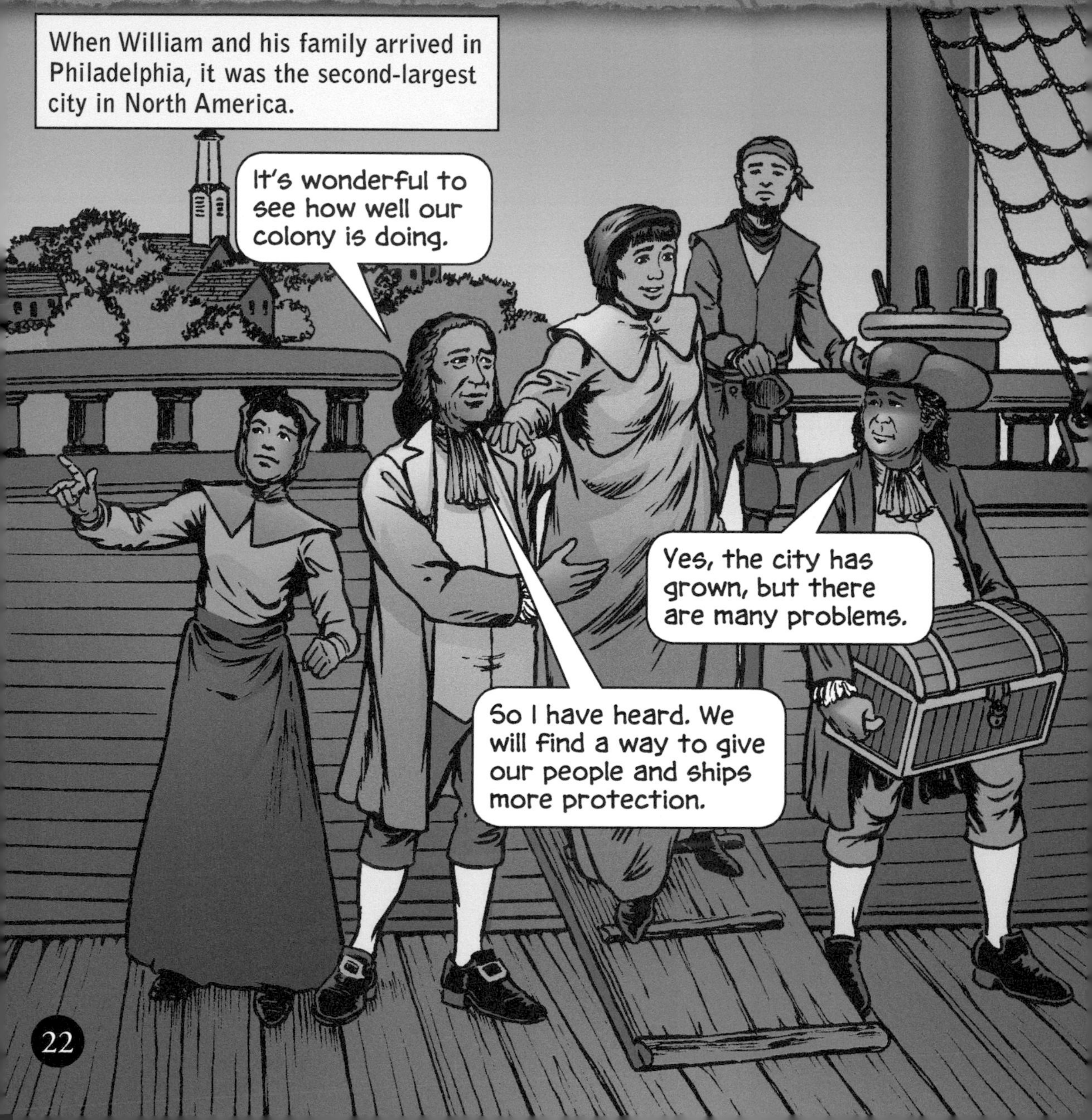
When William and his family arrived in Philadelphia, it was the second-largest city in North America.
It's wonderful to see how well our colony is doing.
Yes, the city has grown, but there are many problems.
So I have heard. We will find a way to give our people and ships more protection.

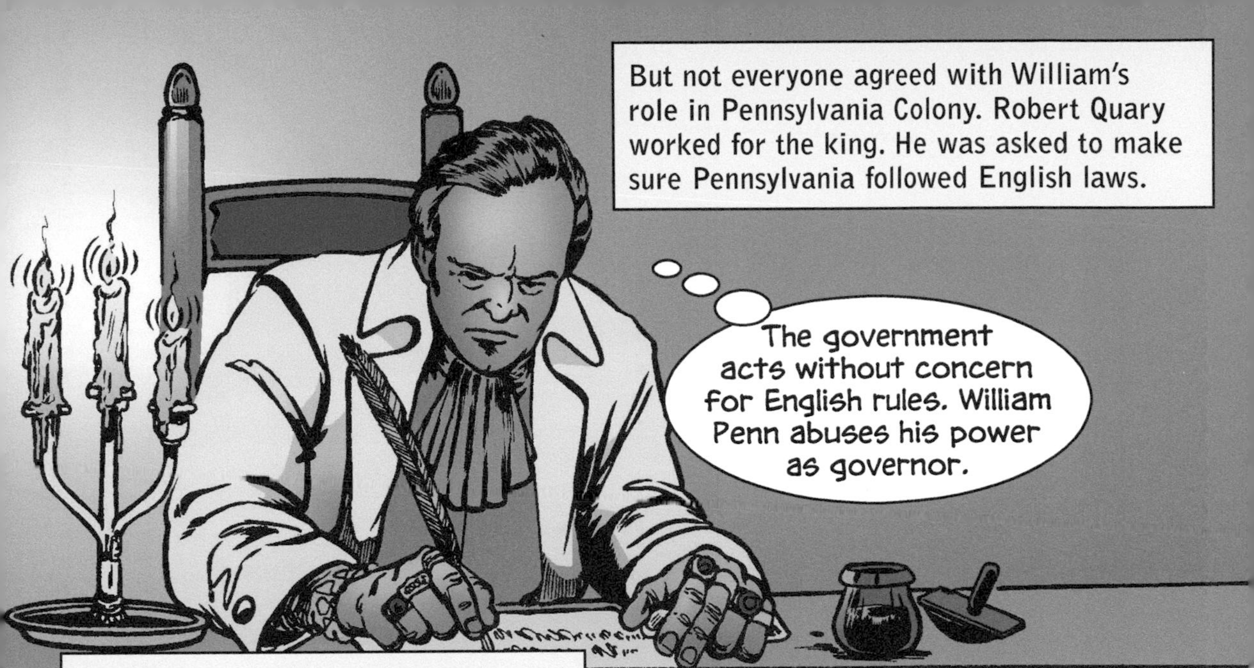

But not everyone agreed with William's role in Pennsylvania Colony. Robert Quary worked for the king. He was asked to make sure Pennsylvania followed English laws.
The government acts without concern for English rules. William Penn abuses his power as governor.

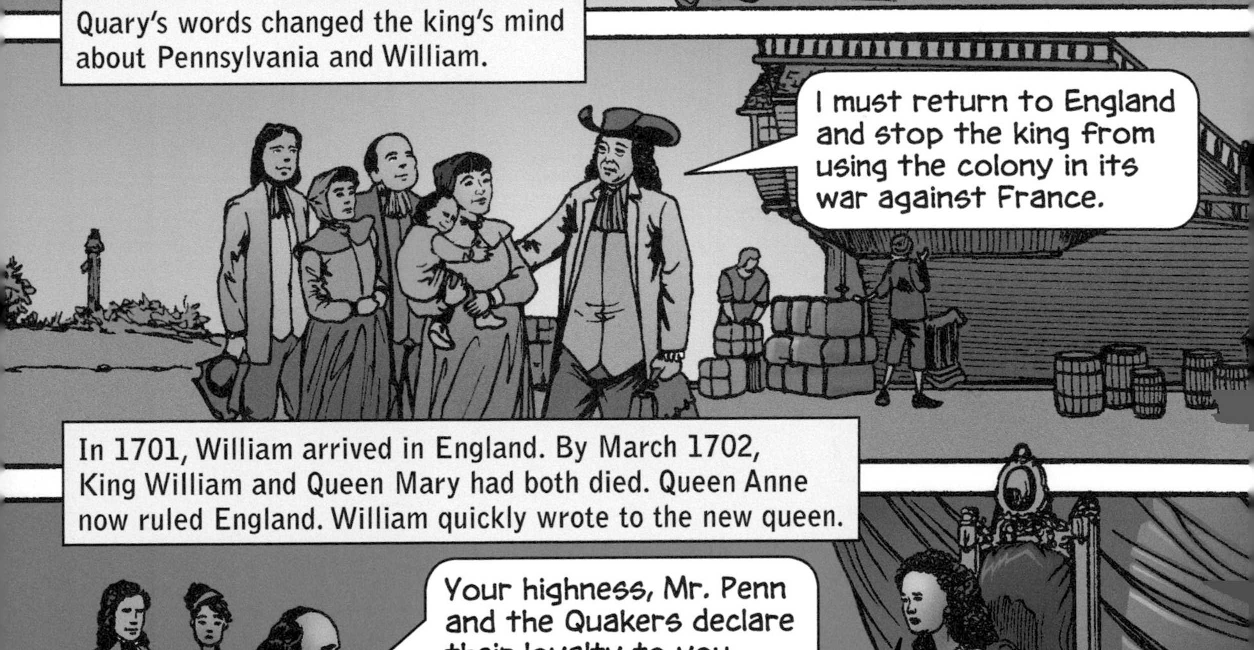

Quary's words changed the king's mind about Pennsylvania and William.
I must return to England and stop the king from using the colony in its war against France.

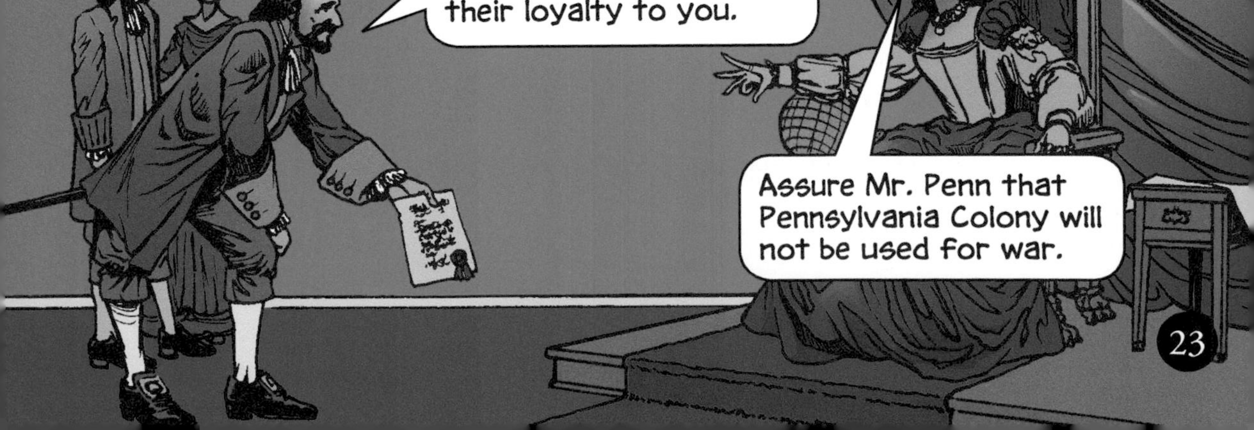

In 1701, William arrived in England. By March 1702, King William and Queen Mary had both died. Queen Anne now ruled England. William quickly wrote to the new queen.
Your highness, Mr. Penn and the Quakers declare their loyalty to you.
Assure Mr. Penn that Pennsylvania Colony will not be used for war.

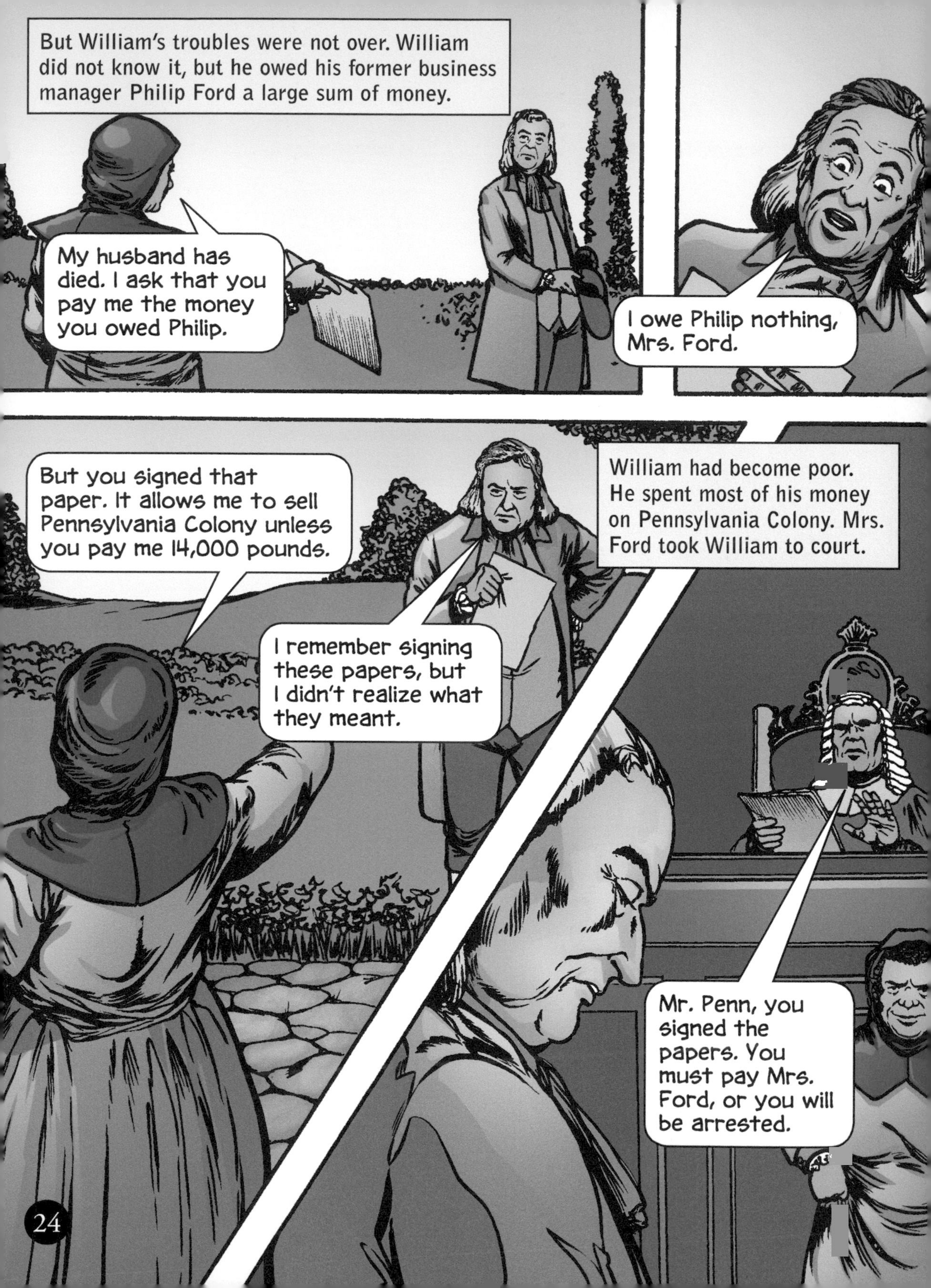

But William's troubles were not over. William did not know it, but he owed his former business manager Philip Ford a large sum of money.
My husband has died. I ask that you pay me the money you owed Philip.
I owe Philip nothing, Mrs. Ford.
But you signed that paper. It allows me to sell Pennsylvania Colony unless you pay me 14,000 pounds.
I remember signing these papers, but I didn't realize what they meant.
William had become poor. He spent most of his money on Pennsylvania Colony. Mrs. Ford took William to court.
Mr. Penn, you signed the papers. You must pay Mrs. Ford, or you will be arrested.

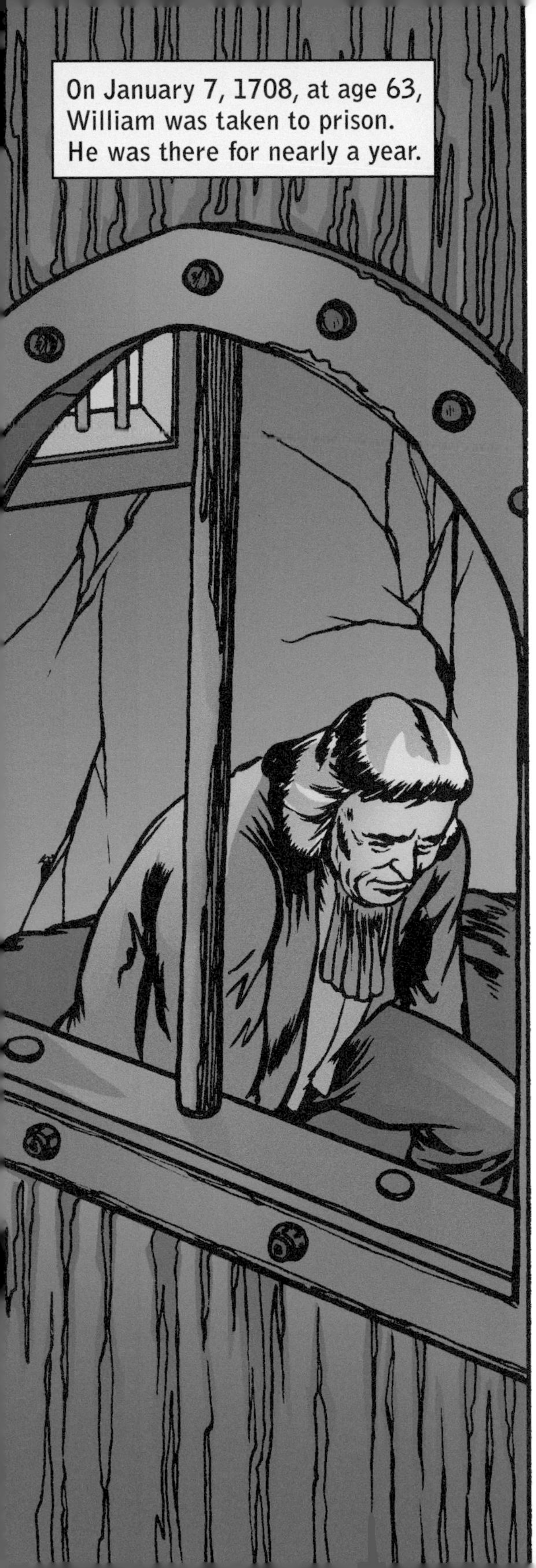
On January 7, 1708, at age 63, William was taken to prison. He was there for nearly a year.

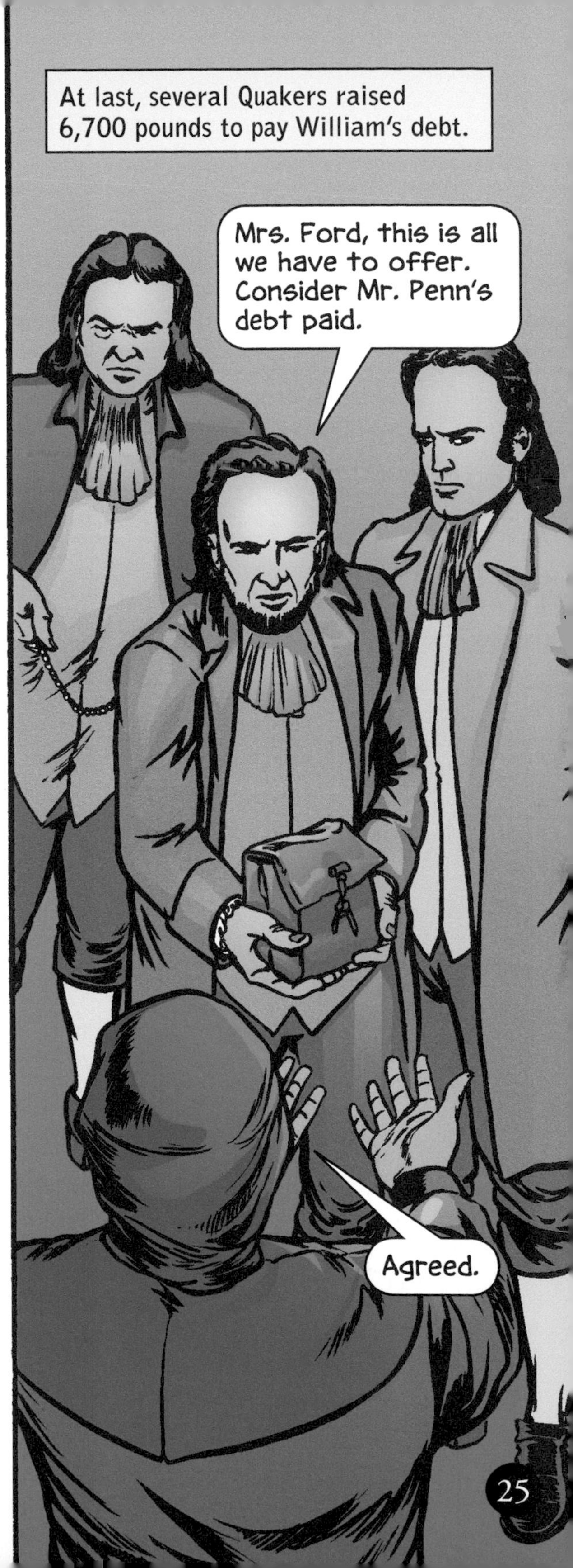
At last, several Quakers raised 6,700 pounds to pay William's debt.
Mrs. Ford, this is all we have to offer. Consider Mr. Penn's debt paid.
Agreed.

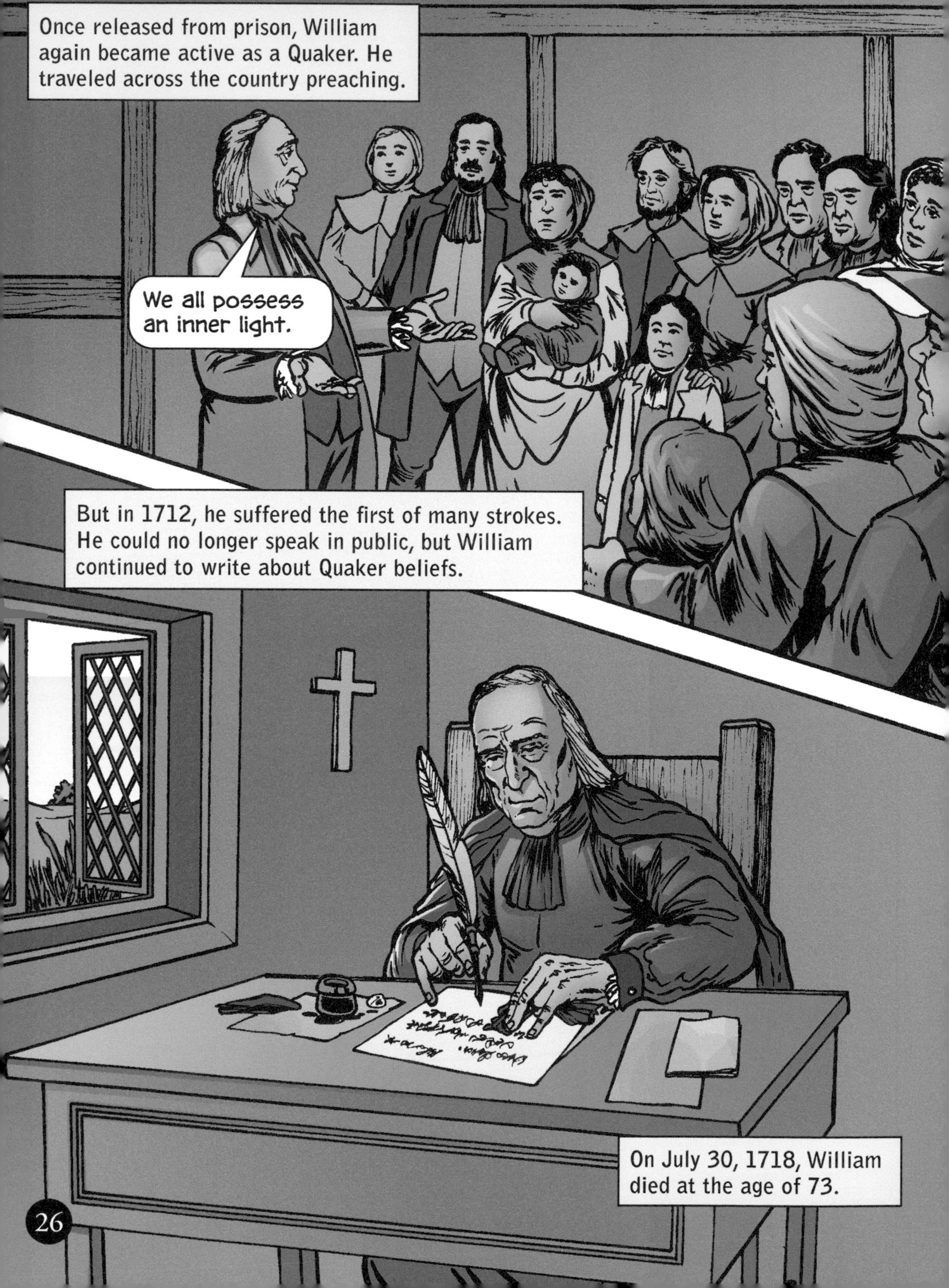

Once released from prison, William again became active as a Quaker. He traveled across the country preaching.
We all possess an inner light.
But in 1712, he suffered the first of many strokes. He could no longer speak in public, but William continued to write about Quaker beliefs.
On July 30, 1718, William died at the age of 73.

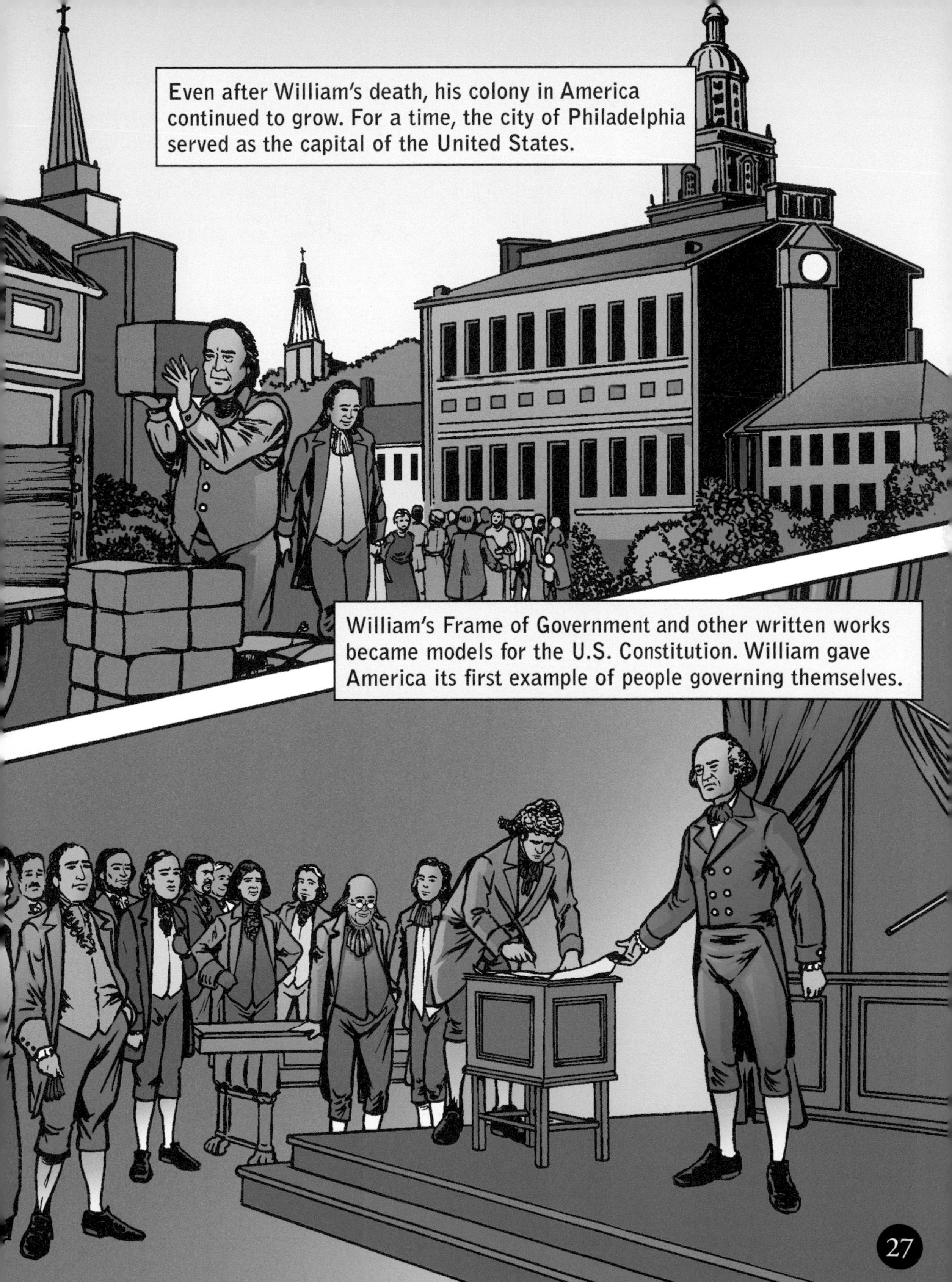
Even after William's death, his colony in America continued to grow. For a time, the city of Philadelphia served as the capital of the United States.
William's Frame of Government and other written works became models for the U.S. Constitution. William gave America its first example of people governing themselves.

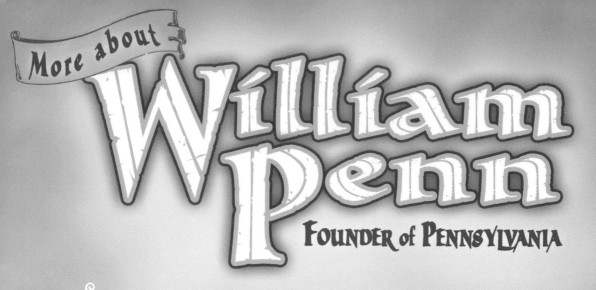

More about William Penn

FOUNDER of PENNSYLVANIA

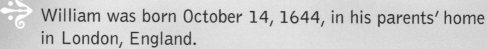

- William was born October 14, 1644, in his parents' home in London, England.

- Quakers were also known as the Religious Society of Friends. They were very friendly people, and they tried to be kind to everyone they met.

- During William's time, Quakers were easy to recognize. They wore plain clothes with no fancy ruffles or trim. Quakers also used words such as "thee" and "thou" instead of "you" and "your."

- William and his first wife, Gulielma, had six children. Five of them died when they were young. William had seven children with his second wife, Hannah. Three of them died at early ages.

- King Charles II chose the name Pennsylvania for William's colony. "Penn" meant "great" and "sylvania" meant "forest." The king also wanted to honor William's father by using "Penn" in the name. But William thought people would believe that he selfishly named the land after himself. Instead, William hoped to call the land New Wales.

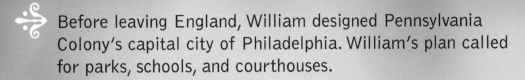 Before leaving England, William designed Pennsylvania Colony's capital city of Philadelphia. William's plan called for parks, schools, and courthouses.

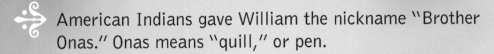 American Indians gave William the nickname "Brother Onas." Onas means "quill," or pen.

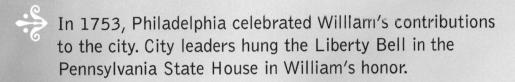 In 1753, Philadelphia celebrated William's contributions to the city. City leaders hung the Liberty Bell in the Pennsylvania State House in William's honor.

Today, a 37-foot-tall statue of William Penn stands atop Philadelphia's city hall. It is the tallest statue on any building in the world.

Glossary

assure (uh-SHUR)—to promise something

colony (KOL-uh-nee)—an area of land settled and governed by another country

estate (ess-TATE)—a large area of land, usually with a house on it

pound (POUND)—a unit of money used in England

Quaker (KWAY-kur)—a member of the Religious Society of Friends, a group founded in the 1600s, that prefers simple religious services and opposes war

treason (TREE-zuhn)—the act of betraying one's country

treaty (TREE-tee)—an official agreement between two or more groups or countries

worship (WUR-ship)—to express love and devotion to a god

Internet Sites

FactHound offers a safe, fun way to find Internet sites related to this book. All of the sites on FactHound have been researched by our staff.

Here's how:
1. Visit *www.facthound.com*
2. Choose your grade level.
3. Type in this book ID **0736865012** for age-appropriate sites. You may also browse subjects by clicking on letters, or by clicking on pictures and words.
4. Click on the **Fetch It** button.

FactHound will fetch the best sites for you!

Read More

Boothroyd, Jennifer. *William Penn: A Life of Tolerance.*
Pull Ahead Books. Minneapolis: Lerner, 2007.

Gillis, Jennifer Blizin. *William Penn.* American Lives.
Chicago: Heinemann, 2005.

Hintz, Martin. *The Pennsylvania Colony.* American Colonies.
Mankato, Minn.: Capstone Press, 2006.

Rau, Dana Meachen, and Jonatha A. Brown. *Pennsylvania.*
Portraits of the States. Milwaukee: Gareth Stevens, 2006.

Bibliography

Bronner, Edwin B. *William Penn's Holy Experiment: The
Founding of Pennsylvania, 1681–1701.* New York: Temple
University Publications, 1962.

Penn, William. *The Papers of William Penn.* Philadelphia:
University of Pennsylvania Press, 1981–1987.

Index